CRICKET IN THE WEB

UNIVERSITY OF
NEW MEXICO PRESS
ALBUQUERQUE

Cricket
in the Web

The 1949
Unsolved Murder
that Unraveled
Politics in
New Mexico

PAULA MOORE

First paperbound printing, 2009
Paperbound ISBN: 978-0-8263-4342-0

Library of Congress Cataloging-in-Publication Data

Moore, Paula, 1942–
Cricket in the web : the 1949 unsolved murder that
unraveled politics in New Mexico / Paula Moore.
p. cm.
Includes bibliographical references and index.
ISBN 978-0-8263-4341-3 (cloth : alk. paper)
1. Coogler, Cricket, 1930–1949.
2. Murder—New Mexico—Las Cruces—History.
I. Title.
HV6533.N4M66 2008
364.152'3092—dc22

2008001104

Book design and type composition by Melissa Tandysh
Composed in 10.75/14.25 Minion Pro
Display type is Kinesis Std
Cover photograph: Ovida "Cricket" Coogler, *El Paso
Herald-Post*, MAY 6, 1949, courtesy Scripps News
Service.
Cover design by Felicia Cedillos

Contents

List of Illustrations

Preface

Ovida "Cricket" Coogler, an undersized and edgy eighteen-year-old wait-ress, left the DeLuxe Café on Main Street in Las Cruces, New Mexico, crying. Having spent eight continuous hours downtown, drinking and wandering among cafés and bars, she refused several rides home and walked unsteadily out into the wee hours of a very dark, cool morning on March 31, 1949.

When her body was found weeks later, the significance of the case began to ripple out, merging here and there with the edges of other criminal cases. Along the way, political corruption was exposed, one political party's twenty-six-year hold on state government came to an end, a state police chief and a county sheriff were unseated, the reputation of various judges and policemen were tarnished, and New Mexico became a theater for the newly emerging civil rights laws. All of these outcomes originated from the death of that one diminutive teenage girl.

The Cricket Coogler case brought a spotlight of attention to the area. The unbridled illegal gambling network, which had been quietly slipping under the control of underworld characters from the Midwest and East Coast, began to squirm. Because certain key law-enforcement and other state officials were paid under the table, certain gambling houses had enjoyed protection from raids and forced closures.

New Mexico's wide-open spaces* made it easier for an illegal gambling/

---

* In the 1940s, New Mexico, geographically the fourth-largest state in the nation, was still so sparsely populated that it was deemed an appropriate place for research and test-ing of the deadliest weapon ever devised. The first atomic bomb was developed at the Los Alamos National Laboratory in the north-central part of the state, and its first test detonation occurred in July 1945 at White Sands Proving Grounds in the southern part, approximately a hundred miles from Las Cruces. If things went horribly wrong with the bomb, it was supposed the fewest possible Americans would be harmed. Gordon Owen, *Las Cruces, New Mexico, 1849–1999: Multicultural Crossroads.*

vice network to thrive. In 1942 one single FBI agent was responsible for the entire state of more than 120,000 square miles, and in 1949 only a handful of agents were yet available. The only two police radio stations were both in the northern half of the state—one at Santa Fe and one at Albuquerque—and teletype was the primary means of communication to other law enforcers around the state. Of about fifty state police officers, only two were stationed in Las Cruces. This scant coverage, as well as favorable access to some politicians, may explain why Al Capone chose to own New Mexico ranch land, and why Bugsy Siegel was considering New Mexico an attractive site for his "gambling Mecca." The southern edge of New Mexico was particularly attractive because it bordered both the state of Texas and the state of Chihuahua, Mexico. In 1949, this stretch of southern New Mexico developed an atmosphere of "anything goes," especially if one had the protection of friends in law enforcement.

Las Cruces, with a current population of more than 75,000, is now the second-largest city in the state of New Mexico. Set along the Rio Grande, in a fertile valley overlooked by the majestic Organ Mountains, Las Cruces recently has been named one of the best places in the nation to do business and to retire. But at the time of the Coogler case a half century ago, Las Cruces was a small town where nearly every one of its 15,000 or so residents knew, or at least knew of, almost everyone else. The town was shaken by the violent death of one of its young women. Theories flew. Suspicions rotated around the sheriff, a football star, some state politicians, a tavern owner, a bank teller, a taxi driver, a truck driver, a farmer, members of the state police, a soldier, and some of Cricket's male friends. The torture of a black suspect in an effort to coerce his confession to the murder of Cricket Coogler brought the FBI into the case.

And, largely because of voter rebellion against political corruption exposed by the Cricket Coogler case, the state's Republican Party was able to overcome Democratic Party dominance and, for the first time since 1935, elect a governor and reclaim many other government offices statewide.

The Coogler case has outlasted the temporary period of attention that any local, unsolved murder engenders—partly because it still contains the elements of mystery, conflict, powerful persons, fear, tangled sexual involvements, and politics.

Reporters have continued to write feature articles about the Coogler case for five decades, but researchers are quick to discover that even in the twenty-first century, the subject of what happened to her—and what happened because of her death—continues to evoke sensitive and emotional reactions. From a distance of more than fifty years, many people refuse even marginal comment. Most of those mentioned in connection to the case have died, but hundreds of their descendants still live in the state, with extended families naturally bound by loyalty.

In the late 1980s, I was in the audience as novelist Tony Hillerman addressed the Rio Grande Historical Association at New Mexico State University, reading the opening pages of his essay-in-progress about the Cricket Coogler case. From his opening line, my obsession with the case was ignited.

A few persons would talk with me under the strictest anonymity, and those requests have been respected. Some voices are presented here for the first time.

In 1949, at least a dozen witnesses gave varying accounts of Cricket Coogler's last evening in downtown Las Cruces. Events thereafter unfolded so rapidly that it is difficult to keep track of them. Hearings and trials sometimes overlapped. Appendix I provides a possible timeline for Cricket Coogler's evening of March 30–31, 1949, and a chronology of events during the succeeding two years.

Abbreviations

The following abbreviations are used in parenthetical documentation notes throughout the text:

AJ	*Albuquerque Journal*
AI	Author's Interview
DP	Papers of William B. Darden, Darden Law Firm, P.A., Las Cruces, NM
EPHP	*El Paso Herald-Post*
EPT	*El Paso Times*
LCB	*Las Cruces Bulletin*
LCC	*Las Cruces Citizen*
LCSN	*Las Cruces Sun-News*
NARA1–NARA7	National Archives and Records Administration, Department of Justice, Federal Bureau of Investigation File 144–49–7, College Park, MD (see bibliography for detail)
SFNM	*Santa Fe New Mexican*
VI	Interview videotaped in the making of *The Silence of Cricket Coogler* (Trespartes Films, 2000)

1   Cricket's Locale

In an old aerial photograph of the city of Las Cruces, New Mexico, the eye is drawn instantly to the largest and most noticeable structure in 1949—the Doña Ana County Courthouse, a gleaming white symbol of justice. Trials and grand jury hearings were held in its courtrooms, and it contained the county jail. The sheriff's small corner office managed to accommodate a desk for state police business.

Between the courthouse and Main Street, running north–south through the middle of town, was a good-sized canal, the Acequia del Madre (the mother ditch), and bridges across it eased east–west traffic.

During the day, Main Street was a center of industry.* Neighbors visited on sidewalks or across café tables about everyday concerns, like the cost of living. Levi's jeans were advertised for $3.25 and a Chrysler Royal four-door sedan for $2,411. People worried about the polio epidemic, and a few local cases were reported.

The downtown area featured several hotels, including the grand Herndon and the historic Amador Hotel, established in 1850 to serve the

---

* The intersection of Griggs and Main streets was the center of town. Street addresses north or south of that point, as well as east or west, began with 100 in each direction. Main Street addresses north of Griggs held even numbers on the east side of the street, odd numbers on the west. South of Griggs, odd numbers were on the west, even numbers on the east, etc.

stagecoach trade. The rooms in the Amador featured feminine Spanish names: "Dolores," "Margarita," etc. Its kitchen once served as the county jail. Just across from the Rio Grande Theatre, the grounds of St. Genevieve's Catholic Church filled an entire block. The church had stood in that spot for a hundred years, the most heavily attended church in the predominantly Catholic town. The Sprouse-Reitz Building was the oldest brick building in the town. In the 1880s guards had been posted on its roof to watch for hostile Indians.

On Saturday nights, both sides of Main Street could be packed with people—especially during harvest times, when hundreds of Mexican laborers swelled the numbers. Work in the local cotton fields brought them to town—fields that in the 1920s had produced cotton plants high and strong enough that a small child could climb them like a tree.

For decades, the cotton fields and other industries had helped make the town a welcoming place, not only for Mexican migrant workers but also for black settlers. Over half of the founders of the city were of Hispanic descent. All races seemed to work and socialize together with mutual respect and little conflict. A black man owned the imposing Herndon Hotel on Main Street and adjoining properties.

Then came the Depression, with so many people desperate for money. More and more Southerners discovered the rich, cheap land in the Mesilla Valley and moved in, bringing expectations of segregation with them. Discrimination grew with the town. Race became a noticeable issue. Some Hispanics whose Catholic Church records could not prove their U.S. citizenship were sent to Mexico. By 1950, blacks in the entire state of New Mexico numbered about 8,000. Las Cruces schools were suddenly segregated, with Las Cruces Union High for Caucasians and Booker T. Washington for black students (at least until some Booker T. Washington boys were drafted for football at Union High). A black suspect would play a huge role in the Coogler case.

Although black soldiers were entitled to the benefits of education under the GI Bill, only a few were enrolled at New Mexico A&M College on the southern edge of the town. However, many returning Caucasian GIs were enjoying the benefits of the GI Bill. Some were serious students, focused on earning a degree to help them provide for their wives and families, but some had learned to drink well and party hard. In any case, the college crowd was older and worldlier than those of other times. Because the schools back east were glutted with GIs, a variety of out-of-staters sought admission to New Mexico A&M. One particularly wealthy applicant, turned away from the nearby School of Mines in El Paso because he arrived one day late, was driven to A&M by limousine, where he met all deadlines and requirements.

College students looking for nightlife could be found seven nights a week, milling around a dozen downtown bars and all-night cafés, mixing with a surprising percentage of the city's population, even after midnight. When darkness fell in Las Cruces, activities in the county could grow dark as well. Several bars were located on Main Street, such as the rough Del Rio Bar and the Welcome Inn, where fights broke out with unfortunate regularity. One resident, a young paper boy at the time, said he liked to deliver papers to the Del Rio Bar because the paper was only a nickel and he often received a quarter from Del Rio patrons. However, at any hour, he always paused at the door to listen for trouble before he entered, and then he avoided eye contact, moving through the place as quickly as possible.

Gateway Gardens, one block east of Main Street (sometimes called Barncastle's Bar), may have hosted a few fistfights, but it also offered a banquet space for clubs and an outdoor patio for dancing. Within a short drive were other lounges, including some in the adjacent older village of Mesilla, where one who drank too much might be thrown out of a hundred-year-old building.

Not all of the city's liquor establishments had a rough reputation, however. The Amador Hotel contained a popular lounge, and waiters in the little Bow Tie Bar on North Main actually wore bow ties.

Soldiers and civilians working at the army's White Sands Proving Grounds, less than an hour's drive east, were often in town. Another group frequenting downtown Las Cruces included officials from the state capital of Santa Fe, a long 282-mile drive from the north. It was worth the drive for a few of them, so it was rumored, because Las Cruces and the forty-five-mile stretch of land from there to the Mexican border offered a sexual playground, and for some, payoffs to be collected from illegal gambling houses and pocketed without accountability. Today, casinos are dotted all over New Mexico, where gambling is legal on American Indian reservation land. But in 1949, owners of illegal gambling joints and prostitution houses, as in other states, made under-the-table payoffs to lawmen and lawmakers for protection. In New Mexico, the most notorious sites were found along the southern border.

Currently, vehicles heading for El Paso/Juarez use I-25, the north–south freeway. But in 1949, they had to choose one of two old roads (still available) that closely follow the Rio Grande into Texas: Highway 80/85, an extension of Las Cruces's Main Street, takes one through the village of Mesquite, whose old cemetery would suddenly become a focal point in the Cricket Coogler case, and the village of Vado, settled in 1876 by primarily black immigrants from Minnesota. Highway 28, the other route, still passes through the old village of Mesilla and beautiful Stahmann Farms, one of the largest pecan groves in the world, where old tree limbs still meet above the road to provide a tunnel of shade for more than a mile. Highway 28 also takes one through the village of La Mesa, with its famous Chope's Restaurant and Bar, operated in those days by a wonderfully vivid character named Chope Benavides. The place is still operated by his family. Democratic precinct chairman in La Mesa for decades, Chope was visited by every savvy statewide Democratic candidate who wished to carry Doña Ana County. He understood better than most how the whole network of political power in southern New Mexico operated, and he personally knew most of the players in the Cricket Coogler case.

The hottest stop along Highway 28 south was Anapra (now called Sunland Park), New Mexico, a little town built by the Southern Pacific Railroad in the 1920s to house employees and their families, almost at the point where Doña Ana County meets the state of Texas at El Paso, and the state of Chihuahua at Juarez, Mexico. Frank Ardovino's place was an elegant high-roller draw. And if the desired vice house could not be found on the way to Mexico, it was an easy skip into Juarez, which offered its own. Today, border crossing often entails a wait in line of almost an hour; but in 1949 only a quick declaration of citizenship at an almost invisible border was all that was required.

It was even claimed that gambling could be established without the consent of the business owner. Justice of the peace T. V. Garcia (indicted by the same grand jury convened because of the Cricket Coogler case) denied that the one-armed bandits in his combination office/store in Anapra were his. He maintained that while he was in Santa Fe trying to get a liquor license, an unidentified man, a perfect stranger, presented the five slots to the Garcia store and went away. Garcia said he thought the fellow could have been one of Sheriff Happy Apodaca's men, and that the machines might have been seized in a raid (*LCSN*, April 19, 1949). Sheriff Apodaca denied that and intimated that a possible motive for planting the machines was that Justice of the Peace Garcia had recently fined a relative of an El Paso newsman. Garcia's subsequent application for a liquor license was denied, and later he spent forty-five days in jail for gambling and embezzlement (*LCC*, January 24, 1950).

If one wished to stay in Las Cruces for a night on the town, "making the rounds" was typical—that is, having a drink or two at one place, then moving on to another because it was the hour music began, or because it was the hour the college crowd or the Santa Fe crowd usually congregated there. This spontaneous agenda could be based on restlessness or simply whether one wanted to avoid or catch a certain crowd. A little gambling in the town was available at some of the private and service clubs.

Some effects from the end of World War II contributed to this nighttime traffic. For some, euphoria that the war was over mixed with a compulsion to live every moment to the fullest. The war had hammered home how precious life was, how final death was. Rules of all kinds loosened. Ordinary townspeople found themselves caught up in the lax atmosphere and convenient access to alcohol, gambling, and sex.

Milder entertainment could be found at downtown movie houses. On the critical evening of March 30, 1949, the Rio Grande Theatre, the oldest two-story adobe theatre in the United States, offered Burt Lancaster and Yvonne de Carlo in *Criss Cross*. Another 1949 release, *Flamingo Road*, starred Joan Crawford as an ambitious waitress who marries a politician and is threatened by a corrupt and very powerful sheriff.

Ironically, March 30, 1949, fell in the middle of the Catholic season of Lent—a period of forty days prior to Easter Sunday in which Catholics are supposed to enter a time of sorrowful reflection marked by three common practices: prayer (justice toward God), fasting or the sacrifice of a favorite food or pastime (justice toward self), and charitable offerings (justice toward neighbors). Unfortunately, a few persons were headed into downtown Las Cruces on the evening of March 30, 1949, seeking excess and intending to avoid justice of any kind.

2 Cricket

By nine-thirty on Wednesday evening, March 30, 1949, Cricket Coogler seemed already to be having a bad night. It would become, horribly, the worst of her life.

According to witnesses, she finished a shift at the DeLuxe Café on Main Street at three o'clock in the afternoon. She hung around downtown awhile, although her home was only a couple of blocks west. The DeLuxe, open twenty-four hours, seven days a week, was a long, narrow café, about twenty feet wide and fifty feet long back to the kitchen wall, with a row of booths along the south wall, one row of tables for four in the center, and a counter with stools and serving space along the north wall. Customers could select jukebox music from each booth. Up front, by the entry, a glass case served as the cash-register table. At the back, the cook could be glimpsed through a narrow pass-through opening to the kitchen. Cricket had only recently begun working at the DeLuxe.

Although slacks were becoming fashionably acceptable, Cricket typically wore dresses, complemented by high-heeled shoes in a variety of colors. Cricket was petite—some people said tiny—weighing as little as ninety pounds. As she left her home about seven in the evening, Cricket told her mother she had a dinner date. She did not say with whom.

Cricket lived with her mother Ollie and twin brother Willie. Her two sisters were married and living elsewhere. In 1943 the family had moved to Las Cruces from Cottondale, Florida—perhaps due to the tuberculosis of

Cricket's father Ben, who died only one year later when Cricket was fourteen. Cricket then dropped out of Union High School and began working as a waitress in several downtown cafés. The Tortugas Café, incorporating the Greyhound bus station, was the place she worked the longest. Why she left the Tortugas for a job at the DeLuxe is uncertain, but she had been known to take off, unannounced, for a few days, even a few weeks, and that alone could have been reason to fire her. Nevertheless, Cricket seemed to drift back to the Tortugas again and again, where some of her friends still worked. The common concerns of her classmates, like geometry and history, cheerleading and baton twirling, no doubt seemed of less value to Cricket than a paycheck. Her wages from café work were minimal, but her family could use any extra money she provided. It was assumed that Cricket was paid by men for sex, although no one had the indiscretion to state that in public.

Some said the nickname "Cricket" came from the sound of her clicking high heels; but a childhood friend says the nickname was hers as a child, because from the beginning she was so small and always on the move. She was no wallflower. Cricket was variously described as vivacious, outgoing, confident, but also moody and uppity. Often, a sad story about her love life edged into conversations with customers. Border patrolman Sylba Bryant's work involved the checking of buses for illegal migrants, and he therefore spent many hours, day and night, waiting for buses at the Tortugas Café. There he regularly observed Cricket for more than a year and described her as "a happy-go-lucky seventeen-year-old who dated just about anybody who came in—didn't draw many lines . . . kind of irresponsible" (VI). Some Tortugas customers appreciated Cricket's sharp, prompt comebacks. She had an "I know who I am—now who are you?" attitude, unusual in so young a girl from so small a town. Cricket also occasionally displayed a hot, sometimes violent, temper (AI).

In 1948, one young admirer, taxi driver Art Marquez, visited the DeLuxe Café at every possible opportunity whenever he knew Cricket, whom he called "Ovie," was working. Sometimes he went into her café to pick up customers for Taxi Number Nine. Art teased Cricket about her accent and was charmed by a little giggle with which Cricket often began a conversation. He tried to work up the courage to ask her out, but she always seemed so much older and wiser, hanging out with law-enforcement and other officials, and he was very young and intimidated by the company she kept.

He nevertheless was about to succeed in arranging a date with her when he joined the army and went off to Japan in January 1949. Ovie agreed that when he returned, they would go out together. Returning to Las Cruces in 1950, Art went directly to the DeLuxe Café with plans to follow up with Ovie Coogler, who had been on his mind during his whole tour of duty. The manager shocked him with the news that Cricket was dead. Art said he left the café and for a time walked in numbness around the downtown area. "She was so pretty," he still remembers wistfully. "I loved the name Ovida" (AI).

Friends of Cricket said she had dated at least one state official. Co-worker Katie Etherton worried about that and tried to counsel Cricket on several occasions, but according to a 1999 videotaped interview, Katie said Cricket

> had gotten into a bad crowd, that Santa Fe crowd, and they had her believing everything they said, and she wouldn't listen to her folks and she wouldn't listen to me. . . . She never went with anybody her own age. She thought she was older than she was, and she thought she was traveling in high company. . . . She always said "I can't tell you his name."

Cricket reportedly went out not only with some politicos from Santa Fe but also local working men—men from White Sands Proving Grounds, soldiers from El Paso's Fort Bliss, and local men. According to her mother, Cricket had dated bus driver Lauren Welch, businessman Jack Baird from Deming, and taxi driver Joel Coffey, the nephew of Taxi Number Nine owner Clay Cole (DP).

The word "date," however, was too mild a term to describe what was going on between Cricket Coogler and at least a few men. Darker stories about her dates were abundant. A Las Cruces dry cleaner told reporters he had been cleaning Cricket's clothes for years, and they were sometimes thoroughly bloody. Sadomasochistic sex and/or brutal men in alcoholic rages could have accounted for some of the blood on Cricket's clothes, and even her death. Border patrolman Sylba Bryant remembered that not long before her disappearance, as Cricket served him in the café, he noticed that the side of her head was banged up and she was complaining about a shoulder. He said he asked her whether some man had given her a hard time, and she answered, "Hell no, I just got mad and jumped out of the car" (VI). About two weeks later, she was dead. The nature of his question, assuming that a man had hit Cricket even before posing it, illuminates a typically condescending attitude toward Cricket, with many in the town murmuring, "What did you expect?" when they learned about her death.

Cricket's blunt answer to Bryant's question—that she jumped from a car—could have come from bravado in an effort to protect her dignity. She no doubt recognized the disdain many townspeople exhibited toward her. Unfortunately, her answer also could have been the simple truth. The story that Cricket routinely jumped out of cars was firmly attached to her and was continually repeated. It sounds a bit absurd, but evidently Cricket was spirited enough, and reckless enough, to jump more than once from a moving car. Perhaps she jumped from one early on the morning of March 31, 1949.

Other evidence of Cricket's reckless participation in dangerous activities had surfaced a couple of years earlier. In late 1946 or early 1947, two college students, both of them veterans on the GI Bill, were studying in their temporary dorm room in a barracks-type building. When they answered a knock at the door about nine in the evening, a rather disheveled young woman told them she needed help and a ride into town. They agreed and asked if she wanted to be taken to the sheriff's office or police. She said no; she wanted to be taken to the Tortugas Café. She didn't say much during the ride, but they gathered she had been assaulted in the desert, abandoned, and had walked toward the campus. They said the girl was Cricket Coogler. At the time, the students assumed she was in her twenties, but she might have been as young as fifteen. Even then, Cricket apparently was willing to endure violence without reporting it—even after abandonment in the desert. In need of aid and comfort, she did not ask to be taken home. She depended instead on someone at the Tortugas Café.

One reliable friend was Josephine Talamantes, who had been Cricket's co-worker at the Tortugas Café. On the evening of Sunday, March 27, 1949, only three days before her disappearance, Cricket and "Josie" made the short trip to El Paso, Texas/Juarez, Mexico. About six that Sunday evening, a street photographer snapped a picture of Cricket and Josie crossing the San Jacinto Plaza in El Paso. The caption under the photograph, published after her death, says that Cricket was wearing a blue-gray suit and red shoes— eerily, the same basic outfit she wore three days later when she died. Her long nails were painted a vivid shade. The attitude conveyed by the photo is clear: a lifted chin, hair pulled back into a severe and sophisticated style that made her look much older than her eighteen years. Her step appears proud, a little defiant. One hand rests on her stomach. Around her neck is a black scarf, and a black purse hangs from her arm by its strap. Three nights later, Cricket chose an oxblood leather purse to match borrowed shoes.

Josie Talamantes said she and Cricket hailed a cab to cross the Mexican border for dinner and a drink, then came back to El Paso's Green Frog Café at 327 North Organ. According to Josie, a dark, husky soldier talked with Cricket and danced with her several times. About nine o'clock the girls headed toward a bus station, but the bus for Las Cruces had just left, so they returned to the Green Frog. When they discovered their previous booth was occupied, the dark, husky soldier invited the girls to sit at his table with him and his friends. The same soldier accompanied the girls to the bus station about midnight, where he had a brief talk with Cricket at the doorway. The street photo of Cricket and Josie was traced to a Phoenix studio after the photographer's stub was found in the black patent-leather purse Cricket had been carrying at the time the picture was snapped. An undisclosed nickname, believed to be that of the soldier, was written on the picture stub. As the girls arrived back in Las Cruces, Josie Talamantes headed for the taxi stand, but Cricket said she wanted something to eat first. The last words from Cricket to her friend were, "Josie, do you have enough money for taxi fare home?" (*EPHP*, May 30, 1949).

Josie Talamantes, shortly thereafter married to a man named Johnson, would find herself on a witness stand the following year, saying she had indeed refused to serve a black man in the Tortugas Café—a man who was jailed on suspicion of murdering her friend Cricket, a man who had also been Cricket's customer, a man who claimed he had never been refused service at the Tortugas.

Concerning Cricket's Sunday evening in El Paso and Juarez, a New Mexico state patrolman spoke with an employee at El Paso's Hotel Angelus, about a block away from the Green Frog, but neither the questions nor the answers were reported (*EPHP*, May 30, 1949). However, the reason for those questions must have been an effort to determine whether Cricket Coogler and a soldier entered that hotel at any time on the evening in question.

Corinne Massingale, another Las Cruces waitress, said she herself had a date with the same husky Fort Bliss soldier on March 27, 1949, but he failed to show. Corinne was apparently jilted on the twenty-seventh, because the soldier met Cricket Coogler at the Green Frog Café in El Paso. Corinne must have given the soldier a rain-check date, because she said she was with him in Las Cruces on the very evening Cricket disappeared—March 30, 1949. Corinne said he left for El Paso on a Greyhound bus at 1:30 a.m. and she watched him ride away. Fort Bliss officials found no soldier on their roster listed under the name the soldier had given the girls, and he was never located (*EPHP*, June 1, 1949).

Even if Cricket Coogler was grappling with some serious problems, her life was not all negative: an attractive appearance, health, youth, good friends, a lifetime of choices ahead, the attention of an array of men and the promises of some. Cricket had the spunk and the will to survive a great deal. Yet, that evening she commented when a spilled drink threatened her suit, "I'll never live to wear it again anyway" (*EPT*, October 31, 1982).

Cricket may have somehow anticipated her fate, but she would not have imagined that her name would become a household word in nearly every city, town, and village in the state of New Mexico and in El Paso, Texas, and that it would command national attention in *Time* magazine and the *New York Times*. Nor would she have dreamed that for decades, her name would rattle the nerves and the consciences of the man or men responsible for her death, as well as those who aided in a cover-up of the crime. And what would she have thought of writer Tony Hillerman's speculation that had it not been for the death of petite little Cricket Coogler and the tangled and bizarre aftermath of that death, Santa Fe, New Mexico, might have become the gambling capital of the nation? And if that had happened, would Las Cruces have then become a sort of Reno (VI)?

On the night of March 31, 1949, Cricket Coogler in some ways was doing what many young women her age had always done—that is, making some terrible choices, following reckless ambition, ignoring common sense, looking for escape in alcohol, experimenting, considering the physical body temporarily expendable. But in other ways, Cricket was doing what very few young women her age would do. She had pushed the edges of dangerous experiences, and she had pushed her luck past the odds for several years.

Thrust from a home apparently dominated by a father in ill health who may have given her little approval or affection, Cricket entered the working world much too early and was drawn into a life with very late hours and almost no boundaries. If her own father withheld approval, the approval of any older man could have become a driving mission. Added to this was the heady experience of being sought after by men with money and power. Although she might have been developing quickly the maturity and rock-hard shell that could allow sexual encounters to be taken lightly, she could not yet manage this consistently in the spring of 1949. More than one person reported that on the night she died, Cricket cried openly about one man and told a taxi driver over the phone that he knew damned well she loved him.

Cricket apparently developed some meaningful relationships with a few men. One older man reportedly wanted to marry her, and an innocent young admirer mentally took her with him overseas during the war. She once confided in a male friend that she thought more of Rosey N. (a former bus ticket agent at the Tortugas Café) than anyone else (NARA1).

She was so very young.

3   Sheriff Alfonso Luchini "Happy" Apodaca

Law enforcement in Doña Ana County, and Las Cruces as its county seat, centered on its handsome sheriff, Alfonso Luchini Apodaca, better known as "Happy." No county could ask for a more fascinating, colorful, and outrageous character than Happy Apodaca. He had friends in high places and knew how to entertain them.

A solid, well-groomed man with a hearty laugh and handshake, Apodaca occasionally wore a trim mustache, after the style of Clark Gable, and a cowboy hat. His mix of humor, charm, and confident good looks was used to great advantage with women. Several observers expressed that less tactfully. One described him as overbearing, macho, and crude, but another said he was a fair man and a good friend. He could appear quite good natured, and more than one person has said they could not help but like him. He once used the campaign slogan "If I can't help you, I sure ain't gonna hurt you" (AI).

One aspect that seemed to endear Apodaca to some was an unusual and genuine capacity to forgive and forget, even toward some people who might be defined as enemies. He apparently expected others to display a similar capacity. One might assume that Apodaca would not speak civilly to any member of the county grand jury who recommended his removal from office, but that was not true. Years after the case, he had coffee occasionally with grand jury member R. A. Durio, showing up with candy for Durio's young son and an invitation to let the boy play with the buttons in his car. Russell Soper, another member of that jury interviewed around 1999 for a video, said Happy would approach him cheerfully, also years after the case, with "Soper, you're the s.o.b. who put me in prison." Soper would reply, "No, Happy, you did that yourself." And Happy would laugh. There seemed in Apodaca's mind a peculiar sense of political give and take that would allow some people a good deal of slack and others none whatsoever. Happy Apodaca was a paradox.

His reputation for continually chasing women, and for using force when his charm failed, prompted many parents to extract promises from their daughters never to get into a car with Sheriff Apodaca. His power was fearsome, and most people in the county tried not to cross him, especially if he had been drinking. At his request, and reportedly in his presence, Cricket had entertained some of his friends from the state capital.

Cricket Coogler definitely knew Sheriff A. L. "Happy" Apodaca. Her mother told reporter Walt Finley:

Cricket has ridden in his car several times.

Two or three times when Cricket got out of the car and came into the house, Sheriff Apodaca would get out and visit with his sister-in-law, Beatrice Apodaca [widow of his brother Santiago], who lives in a next-door apartment.

Cricket didn't like Happy. Several times when something was said about him, Cricket would say "I don't like that guy" or I could tell by the way she acted she didn't like him. (*EPHP*, May 16, 1949)

Like him or not, Cricket Coogler and Happy Apodaca would be linked forever.

Born September 12, 1913, Happy Apodaca, the fourth of ten boys, grew up in a cattle-ranching/farming family in Garfield, New Mexico, north of Las Cruces, on rich land that backed up to the Rio Grande. FBI archives indicate that one of his brothers, Horacio, had problems of his own with the law. He was charged with a 1937 rape of a twelve-year-old girl in Las Cruces but not prosecuted, allegedly due to his family's political influence. On another occasion, Horacio Apodaca and Willie Luchini were held as suspects in connection with the slaying of Deputy Sheriff Warren Ruiz in a brawl outside a tavern near Hot Springs, New Mexico, in October 1942. After two brief *Sun-News* articles about the case, it faded and was never solved.

Happy Apodaca and his brothers were fiercely competitive with the Gonzales brothers, also of Garfield, trying to outdo each other in sports and any other endeavor.* Happy Apodaca attended Garfield's elementary school from 1920 to 1928, where his grades were below average, his conduct bad. In high school, 1928 to 1933, he played basketball and football and was described by the school superintendent as "sexually minded" (NARA3).

After graduation from Hatch High School in 1933, Apodaca served in the U.S. Marine Corps. He then attended New Mexico A&M College from September 1937 to January 1938, but received no college credits inasmuch as he failed all subjects in freshman agriculture. In 1940 Apodaca married a pretty young woman with the same surname, Antonia Fierro Apodaca of Mesilla, New Mexico, and they had five children (two at the time of the Coogler case).

Apodaca was a professional and service (USMC) heavyweight boxer, once fighting Billy Conn, who went on to become the light heavyweight champion, 1939–1941 (*LCSN*, October 9, 1949). One Las Cruces acquaintance said Happy invariably greeted him with a couple of left jabs from a boxer's stance, followed by a sharp and painful right to the chest—all in good fun, of course.

From 1938 to 1940, Happy Apodaca had been employed as deputy county clerk of Doña Ana County, working for his brother, county clerk Santiago Apodaca. The succeeding county clerk, Manual Chavez, advised that Happy Apodaca was not a man for law-enforcement work or for a position of trust, inasmuch as when he, Chavez, took office, he discovered a shortage of $2,000. He also found a deed on which ink eradicator had been used to remove the name of Santiago Apodaca's wife, upon Santiago's death, to favor Happy instead. State auditor James Hannah verified to the FBI that Happy Apodaca had removed the name on the deed. The county sheriff at that time, Santos Ramirez, who had known Apodaca all his life, once commented to an FBI agent that Apodaca "drank and chased women, was hot headed, and was not reliable" (NARA3).

Apodaca was more than friendly with the political machine of the Democrats, and at the time New Mexico was virtually a one-party state. He

---

* Rudolfo Gonzales was county sheriff 1965–1970; Tony Gonzales was county sheriff 1975–1978, and Adrian Gonzales ran the Blue Moon Bar at nearby Radium Springs.

had enjoyed his own term in the state government in the early 1940s, when he was employed by the State Bureau of Revenue in Santa Fe (headed at the time by J. O. Gallegos, Senator Dennis Chavez's brother-in-law, prompting speculation that Senator Chavez sanctioned the position for Apodaca). This must have been the season when Apodaca strengthened his political network, and any ties to Senator Dennis Chavez would have been formidable, because Chavez wielded a lion's share of political power in the state. Reporter Walt Finley said he felt that because of Apodaca's power and rumored ties to Senator Chavez and Santa Fe officials, the state police were most reluctant to do any kind of investigation in Doña Ana County (VI). Happy Apodaca was personally acquainted with Lt. Governor Joseph Montoya, corporation commissioner Dan Sedillo, state police chief Hubert Beasley, superintendent of insurance R. F. Apodaca (Happy's brother-in-law), employment security commissioner Benjamin Luchini (a cousin to Happy's mother Teotiste "Tillie" Luchini), comptroller J. D. Hannah, and many others in state offices, not to mention Doña Ana County's Democratic office holders and party workers.

In 1942 Happy Apodaca became a state policeman and immediately made himself conspicuous. His personnel file with the New Mexico State Police, cited in FBI archives, reflected that in September 1942 he was given an indefinite leave of absence after an accumulation of complaints. In each instance, the complaint described was conduct unbecoming an officer. One specific reason for his suspension was a political argument with a Las Cruces man named Dan Williams. (This could have been the same Dan Williams who was president of the college's board of regents and head of the highway department in Doña Ana County.) Apodaca broke Williams's jaw and knocked out one eye, but Apodaca was nevertheless reinstated with the state police in February 1943.

In 1946 Jeanneice Autry, a fourteen-year-old, was excused from both a written test and a driving test by then state policeman Happy Apodaca, who simply took her application and asked her to turn around so he could use her back as a desk. He signed the excuse, then told her to go home and tell her mother to vote for him, as he was running for sheriff (AI).

Apodaca's unorthodox ways continued at election time. Reporter Alice Gruver, already disillusioned after some interviews with Apodaca, said she observed him at a voting place, handing out pint bottles of whiskey to voters (VI).

As Apodaca became sheriff of Doña Ana County early in 1949, he was already well known. People sought his approval because he could fix serious problems and because, conversely, he could create serious problems. He was fiercely loyal to family and friends, and if one of them was crossed, he could be relentless in ensuring payback. It became commonly accepted that traffic or drunk-driving citations, or even greater offenses, could be forgiven if Sheriff Apodaca said so. The city police and many townspeople appeared reluctant to cross him. Sheriff Apodaca apparently expected not only deference, but citywide favors as well. Once he entered an auto-repair shop on Main Street and took some oil for his car, not offering to pay for it. When confronted and asked for payment, he was indignant (AI).

Aside from the favors it dispensed, the sheriff's office had a busy workload in Doña Ana County, which had an amazing record of about one violent death a month, according to the April 7, 1949, *Las Cruces Citizen*.

Sheriff Apodaca generously catered to politicians from Santa Fe when they visited his county, especially longtime friends, those he knew from his stint in the state government offices, or those he knew from his days roaming the state as a state policeman. He reportedly made life easier for these friends while they were in his county, granting their wishes. Russell Allen Soper, a hotel operator in nearby Hatch and a member of the county grand jury that held hearings on the handling of the Coogler case, confirmed on tape that the sheriff's office was a semi-headquarters for politicians, a place where favors were expedited. Some of those favors included procuring girls and alcohol.

Another favorite group of Apodaca's was the football team at the college, particularly one star who had recently turned pro with the Pittsburgh Steelers—Jerry Nuzum—who continued his academic pursuits at A&M in the off-season.

Sheriff Apodaca's deputies included Roy Sandman, a short, heavy-set man who had survived two German prisoner-of-war experiences and had recently married a Las Cruces widow. Sandman abruptly resigned his deputy position in June 1949 and took a position as field agent for the Third Judicial District, attached to the district attorney's office—a position newly created by the legislature. This abrupt job change occurred after the initial two months of the investigation of the death of Cricket Coogler. Former FBI agent Jess Weir told investigating agents that Sandman's hands were tied by Apodaca throughout the investigation of the Coogler case and Sandman never could conduct the investigation as he wished. Whatever their relationship, Sandman and Apodaca would soon be together in prison.

Working closely with Sheriff Apodaca was T. K. Campbell, the area's brand-new district attorney, succeeding W. T. Scoggin Jr., who had stepped up to a judge's bench that would be permanently linked to the Cricket Coogler case. Born in Doña Ana County, the young, arrogant T. K. Campbell, always impeccably dressed, was active in the Chamber of Commerce, American Legion, VFW, and Elks Club. He had married Margaret Slater of Washington, DC, and had earned a Distinguished Flying Cross and other medals as a B-17 pilot in World War II. Some considered him inexperienced and immature, others found him honest and sincere, and still others had an idea he was less than ethical and that he considered himself "God's gift to women" (AI). At the time of the Coogler case, Campbell had been district attorney for only three months.

The offices of the district attorney had two entrances, side by side. The main, marked entrance took a visitor through the office of the secretary; the other opened directly into Campbell's space. The DA's secretary, therefore, sometimes did not know who was talking to Campbell, but one frequent visitor to the DA's office must have been Sheriff Apodaca.

When Campbell's assistant district attorney, E. E. Chavez, resigned as Democratic Party chair, the *Las Cruces Citizen* (January 13, 1949) anticipated Sheriff Happy Apodaca as successor to the party chairmanship, because Happy was

> one of the few Democratic leaders in the county who may be able to reconcile divergent forces within the party and promote more amicable relations between local political powers and those of the same party in the rest of the state and in Santa Fe. Well known in the community by virtue of his work with the state highway patrol for the past decade, and his long residency here, he is said to possess all the attributes of the ideal county chairman.

Someone else, however, gained the position.

As the Coogler case led to revelations of corruption from one end of the state to the other, there came a time, as respected New Mexico political reporter Jack Flynn put it, when a few men saw opportunities to become the governor of New Mexico or a member of the U.S. Congress, and it was time to play real hardball. Interviewed on videotape in the late 1990s, Flynn did not name names about who specifically might play hardball, but however unlikely, Happy Apodaca himself had been mentioned as a possible gubernatorial candidate. Apodaca may have possessed few credentials for a governor, but he understood well the system of political favors. Other possible gubernatorial candidates were District Attorney T. K. Campbell, Senator Dennis Chavez's brother David, and Lt. Governor Joseph ("Little Joe") Montoya, to name a few.

4 Cricket's Last Hours

According to several witnesses, Cricket Coogler's last night on the town included the attentions of more than one man. Her restless movements in and out of downtown bars and cafés that evening are reminiscent of a film in fast-forward mode [see constructed timeline, appendix I]. Finally, around three in the morning, she climbed into a mysterious car driven by an unknown man and was never seen alive again.

One of the men paying attention to Cricket that evening was twenty-six-year-old Luther Mosley, who was enough of a regular at downtown bars and cafés that he was dubbed "Mr. Green Eyes," because he almost always wore glasses with green lenses. His eyes were also a greenish blue. Typically in boots and jeans, Mr. Green Eyes drove a truck for the P. R. Burn Construction Company.

Bob Ash, the DeLuxe Café manager, said the man with the green glasses had been in the café with Cricket a couple of times on the morning of March 30, and waitress Leonora "Shorty" Fischer said she observed Cricket sitting next to Mr. Green Eyes early that evening at the Del Rio, where she said Cricket was ignoring him and they appeared to be angry with each other.

After midnight, several people spotted Cricket with Jerry "Bruiser" Nuzum, a former New Mexico A&M football star who had moved up to professional status with the Pittsburgh Steelers. Married with two children, Nuzum was in Las Cruces during the Steelers' off-season to continue his college coursework under the GI Bill after four years in the U.S. Navy. He enjoyed celebrity status because of his connection with the Steelers. Girls sought him out, some in order to brag about knowing him. Nuzum also worked as a bouncer at the Airport Inn lounge, a position likely resulting from Nuzum's friendship with Sheriff Happy Apodaca. Apodaca had deputized Nuzum, thereby qualifying him as a bouncer.

Exactly what Cricket did from 3:00 p.m., when she finished a shift at the DeLuxe Café, until 7:00 p.m., when she left her home at 116 South Water, is unknown. According to Lauren Welch, who said he had been "going around with Cricket" until late 1948, he and a friend walked out of the DeLuxe Café about 6:15 or 6:30 p.m. on March 30, 1949, and he said he saw Cricket on the corner of May and Main streets, in her waitress uniform. Then he said he went home, and he, his wife, and another couple went to the movies, got back around midnight, and went to bed. Welch left on a bus for Salina, Kansas, the next night, April 1, 1949, at 1:30 a.m. and did not return. His wife told Agent McConnell that she and Lauren separated when they moved from Las Cruces, which could have been the moment he boarded that Kansas-bound bus (NARA1).

If Welch's sighting of Cricket was accurate, she had time for several drinks between 3:00 p.m. and 6:15 p.m., when she went to her home at 116 South Water, freshened up, and changed from her waitress outfit into a gray skirt and a blue and gray plaid jacket. She wore a pair of oxblood pumps her sister Cookie had purchased about four years earlier. (The sisters wore the same size and apparently traded shoes occasionally, even though Cookie lived in Muleshoe, Texas, at the time.) (*EPHP*, May 16, 1949) A matching leather purse was the final accessory. About 7:00 p.m., Cricket told her mother she had a date, but would not say with whom. Cricket then walked back over to Main Street. The city directory listed no telephone number for the Cooglers, so any date was likely arranged by a phone call to the DeLuxe Café or an in-person visit. One visitor may have been Sheriff Apodaca, who later told Ollie Coogler he had seen her daughter on March 30. The weather was nippy, with an expected low of thirty-one degrees that night after a pleasant daytime temperature of sixty-four, but Cricket wore no coat other than her suit jacket. March 30, 1949, was a very dark night, only one night after a new moon. Cricket's mother, finding Cricket's billfold at home, thought it odd she had not put it in the red leather purse.

Cricket evidently went to a bar and ordered another of many drinks she would have that evening. Although underage, Cricket had no problems obtaining liquor that evening, or any other. One bartender said she had been refused liquor service many times at his workplace, not because of her age, but because she was obviously drunk.

Cricket was seen walking unsteadily on Main Street in front of the DeLuxe Café about 8:00 p.m. She entered the café, where Mr. Green Eyes observed her talking to a small man of about 105 pounds in khaki trousers, a white shirt, and a brown or dirty blue hat. On the evening in question, Jerry Nuzum wore khaki trousers and a white T-shirt. But Mr. Green Eyes would not have confused the two. Football player Nuzum could not be described as small, and Green Eyes was to watch Nuzum closely as the evening progressed and eventually confront him face to face at least once.

Nuzum, who had already made many stops on his own appointed rounds that evening, apparently did not come onto the downtown scene until after midnight, when he entered the DeLuxe and saw Cricket Coogler sitting by herself at the counter. In what might have been a flirtatious opening act or revelation of an already established intimacy, Nuzum removed a cigarette from Cricket's hand and put it out. He sat down beside her for a short time. Café manager Bob Ash was on site, and Cricket visited a bit with him. One of the waitresses on duty commented to Ash that Cricket was not as drunk as Nuzum thought she was.

At some point, at the next-door Del Rio Bar, Jerry Nuzum invited Cricket, and possibly Mr. Green Eyes and others, to play shuffleboard. Nuzum and Cricket then went outside together, and after a struggle (some said serious; Nuzum said joking), Nuzum lifted Cricket and attempted to put her in his car. She got away and started back into the café. Mr. Green Eyes, ostensibly with Cricket's best interests at heart and playing the role of rescuer, walked out to confront Nuzum.

Mr. Green Eyes Mosley at first refused to discuss the case with reporters because he said district attorney T. K. Campbell had ordered him to keep his mouth shut. Campbell would not comment regarding that statement. Mosley did eventually tell his story in court and to Walt Finley of the *El Paso Herald-Post* (June 26, 1951):

[I saw] Cricket in the Del Rio bar. [He later pinpointed this to about 11:00 p.m.] She was about to fall off her stool when I saw her. She had knocked over her glass of whisky. I set it up to keep it from dripping on her purse. [When someone warned Cricket that the spill would ruin her new suit, Cricket replied, "I'll never live to wear it again anyway."] (*EPHP*, May 10, 1949)

. . . she went to the rear of the bar and . . . I believe she phoned someone. [She] returned . . . laid her head on the bar, and cried. She said she was in love with someone but knew that someone didn't care anything about her. She asked me what I would do. I told her to forget about it. (*EPHP*, May 12, 1949)

Shorty Fischer confirmed Cricket's romantic anguish. She said Cricket asked her to phone Taxi Number Nine (a local taxi stand cleverly named to include its telephone number, which was the one digit: 9), ask for a specific driver by number, and tell him Cricket loved him because she would not live to tell him herself. Miss Fischer refused (*EPHP*, May 10, 1949).

Cricket decided to make a call herself. About midnight, she was overheard saying into the phone, "You know damn well I love you" (*EPHP*, May 12, 1949). Cricket had dated Joel Coffey, a driver for Taxi Number Nine. Coffey later confirmed that he did receive a phone call from Cricket that night, inviting him to the café, and he declined. She continued instead in the company of Mr. Green Eyes, Luther Mosley, who asked her to go with him to the Tortugas for coffee. Mosley told reporter Walt Finley:

At the Tortugas Café a man and a waitress there refused to serve her because she was drunk. . . . Cricket talked to a Spanish-American cop there while I was paying the check. [City policeman Flores said he saw her there (*EPHP*, June 28, 1951).] [We] returned to the Del Rio . . . Nuzum came in about this time. . . . Nuzum asked [Cricket], "Honey, what's your name?" I could tell Nuzum didn't know Cricket by the way he was talking to her while they were playing shuffleboard. . . . They [walked out of the bar and] got in Nuzum's car. I saw Cricket open the door. When she started to get out, Nuzum grabbed for her but didn't get hold of her. Then Nuzum opened the driver's side door and ran around to catch her. He was talking loud and seemed very angry. Cricket went on back into the bar.

Jerry was standing at the back of his car. I couldn't tell whether [he] was drunk or just [had been] drinking. . . . I told Nuzum that Cricket didn't have to go with him if she didn't want to. He replied, "Listen, fellow, are you looking for trouble? If you are, you had better leave town and leave at once." I told him I never had been made to leave town and didn't think he could make me. (*EPHP*, May 12, 1949, and June 26, 1951)

Mosley had also walked Cricket to the Union Depot, a block from the Tortugas, where they ordered coffee and doughnuts. Seemingly intent on getting some fresh air and food into her, Mosley escorted Cricket back to the Tortugas, where this time the staff did serve coffee and toast to Cricket. Throughout the long evening, Cricket repeatedly said to several people that she was going home as soon as she ate, or as soon as she had one more cup of coffee. But she apparently had no intention of going home.

Luther Mosley finally either gave up or reversed his attempts to sober up Cricket and instead bought her drinks. Mosley and Cricket made a few more short walks between the Del Rio Bar and the DeLuxe Café. Two a.m. found them at the DeLuxe (open all night), sitting on barstools at the counter. Then, apparently rejecting Mosley, Cricket moved to a booth alone, where she was joined once again by Jerry Nuzum. They talked, and then Nuzum went to the telephone. Mosley described it to Walt Finley:

Jerry picked up a phone but I don't know whether he used it or not. He walked outside. . . . I told Cricket when she went outside Nuzum probably would force her to get into his car [again]. . . . (*EPHP*, May 12, 1949, and June 26, 1951)

Cricket ignored this warning, and sure enough, as she went outside, Nuzum again lifted her and moved toward his car. Now it was about 2:30 a.m. This time, DeLuxe manager Bob Ash went out to intervene because he said he heard Cricket call out to him not to let Nuzum take her. Again, this could have been taken as a joke or seriously. Nuzum asked Ash whether he was trying to interfere with his business, and Ash answered that he was not. That exchange sounds a little testy—not a joke at all. Nuzum's car motor was not started. In an odd coincidence, Bob Ash's wife observed this mild altercation from a half block away, as she had just exited a bus at the Tortugas Café/bus station and begun walking toward her husband's workplace. She indicated that Cricket, Nuzum, and Ash seemed to settle down, and all returned to the inside of the DeLuxe.

But Nuzum did not sit down. Instead, he asked to use the telephone again. This time he dialed 2-7, the number of the sheriff's office. There was no answer (it was after midnight), so he asked an operator to get him the police. In a moment, Nuzum was heard asking whether he had the jurisdiction to make an arrest. In Cricket Coogler's hearing, he said that a woman had been causing trouble at the Airport Inn, where Nuzum was a bouncer (*EPHP*, May 11, 1951). Nuzum explained this later by saying he was talking to a dead phone and simply trying to make a big impression with the whole episode (VI).

According to Bob Ash, he and Mrs. Ash left the DeLuxe Café about 2:45, at which time Nuzum was still standing behind Cricket as she sat at the counter (*EPHP*, May 11, 1951). Mosley, still keeping Cricket in his sight almost constantly, said Nuzum then left the café alone and drove off to the south. Resident Stan Riley contradicted the time Nuzum left the café. Riley and waitress Shorty Fischer, whom Riley was driving home, both told Walt Finley they saw Cricket embracing Nuzum outside a Main Street café at 3:00 a.m. (*EPHP*, July 19 and 21, 1949). Nuzum lived only about five minutes away, and his landlady would say he was home at 2:55 a.m. A discrepancy in clocks could be claimed, but those were vital minutes.

After one last refusal of Mosley's offer of a ride home, Cricket left the DeLuxe Café alone. Mosley again paid Cricket's bill and followed her on foot. Mosley said:

She was drunk and I was afraid he [Nuzum] would try to pick her up again—that's why I followed her. . . . She came out of the café and walked north across the street at a signal light. A car was going north and she was about in the middle. I said to Cricket, "Watch that car." She kept walking like she didn't see it. The car slowed down almost to a stop. There were two men in the car as well as I can remember. The men said something to Cricket. I don't know whether she said anything or not.

She walked across the street and past the post office, then south on Church Street. She started running when she turned on Church Street.

Then she fell down. She seemed like she was crying or screaming. I said two or three times "Are you hurt?" She got up and ran on.

Then I saw a car moving slowly towards us [from] the next block. I got to thinking and turned back. I don't know who was in the car. (*EPHP*, May 11, 1951)

Mosley indicated he saw Cricket shortly after 3:00 a.m. talking with the man who possibly was her slayer, wearing a hat and driving a car that was dark brown or possibly dark gray. He said that a few minutes later he saw what might have been the same car turning off Main Street on Church Street. (Note: This was not possible because Main and Church are parallel streets. Perhaps he said "May" Street, not Main Street, which would have fit with the stories of other observers.) Mosley said after that, he went to his room at the Amador Hotel (*EPHP*, May 12, 1949, and May 11, 1951).

Mosley commented that the desk clerk at the Amador Hotel had seen him with Cricket in the Tortugas Café earlier in the night. The desk clerk concurred, but could not recall Mosley's coming into the Amador or going out. She said the thing that impressed her at the Tortugas was that Mosley was gentle with Cricket, trying to get her to eat toast and drink some coffee, putting an arm around her to help her walk as the two left the café (*EPHP*, May 13, 1949).

A couple of years after the event, Mosley told Walt Finley that the color of the car he had initially described as gray or brown was, instead, black. City police were reportedly driving a black car that night. Certainly Mosley was familiar with Nuzum's maroon car, since he "rescued" Cricket from that car earlier in the evening. When Mosley saw car lights approaching Cricket (along Church Street), he said he "got to thinking" and retreated to his hotel. It was convenient for some, especially for Mosley himself, that he claimed not to have seen Cricket enter the car. Maybe Mosley "got to thinking" because he recognized, even feared, the driver and/or passenger. If two men were in the car that almost hit Cricket on Main Street, then two men were likely still in it if she entered that car at Church and Bowman. One who was certain of the color of that car and who was in it was, of course, Cricket Coogler, who ran and stumbled and fell after making her turn onto Church Street, where that car passed her slowly, then made a right turn across her path. Nevertheless, crying or not, she walked toward it and climbed inside.

Football player Jerry Nuzum described his version of the evening of March 30, 1949, to Walt Finley:

I left home about 7:30 p.m. to go to a picture show. I stopped at the Penguin Bar to have a beer. After a couple of beers I went to the Airport Inn. [Later Nuzum recounted a stop at the Legion Bar where he played shuffleboard with Ray Apodaca and left about 10:30.] I returned to the Penguin Bar. Then two girls who had worked at the Airport Inn . . . and I went to the Oasis Bar [on Picacho Avenue, a short drive from downtown]. We had one drink. I went back to the Penguin Bar and played shuffleboard. I decided to drive back to the Airport Inn. When I got there the place was closed. I looked at my watch; it was 1 a.m. I drove back downtown and went to the Elks Club [212 S. Main]. A former officer of the club gave me ten dollars that he said he owed my dad. We were the only ones in the club. I left there about 1:30 a.m. (*EPHP*, May 7, 1949)

Nuzum's rounds then took him to the bar where Cricket Coogler sat:

I drove my car from in front of the Elks Club to the DeLuxe Café [one block north]. I went into the Del Rio Bar where I met Miss Coogler and played shuffleboard with her and a man I never had seen before. We played until the bar closed.

Miss Coogler asked me to take her home. On the way out of the bar we decided to get a cup of coffee. First, we went out to my car.

I was trying to help Miss Coogler get in the car. She told me she didn't need any help. I started around the car. She jumped out . . . and ran into the DeLuxe Café. I walked into the café and told the girl, "The hell with you."

Bob Ash . . . asked me if I was trying to kidnap Miss Coogler. I told him no. I showed him my deputy sheriff identification papers.

I never did sit down. I returned to the Penguin. About a year ago, I worked there as bartender. Some men were playing shuffleboard. I walked behind the bar and mixed a pretty strong drink. I decided I was getting pretty drunk, so I drove home. (*EPHP*, May 7, 1949)

Nuzum said nothing about the heated encounter with Mr. Green Eyes Mosley, describing instead only the one encounter with Bob Ash. And Nuzum said nothing about angry words with Cricket, maintaining he barely knew her and was with her a very brief time that fateful morning.

Mosley said Nuzum left the DeLuxe alone and drove away to the south, but Nuzum said he went only two doors away to the Penguin Bar, so there was as yet no need for driving.

Nuzum lived on Alameda, several blocks northwest of the DeLuxe. His landlady said she was awakened by a car horn honking beneath her window at 2:55 a.m. This would have been Nuzum's obnoxious arrival. Mary Nuzum said she had to help her drunk husband inside (*EPHP*, May 7, 1949).

Two other eyewitnesses downtown that evening were city policemen Reuben Flores and Vicente Lucero, who were on duty together. In a lengthy formal statement given to the press, here is what Patrolman Vicente Lucero said they observed:

> About 3:05 a.m. we saw Miss Coogler in front of the news stand at the corner of Griggs and Main streets. We advised her to go home.
>
> We drove along in the patrol wagon for a few minutes, and then saw her in front of the Western Union office on May Street. It was about 3:10 a.m. We stopped and asked her to let us take her home.
>
> She said she had a ride. She was alone, as she was when we saw her by the news stand, but there was a man following her. We did not recognize him. [This had to be Mosley.]
>
> We went down May, to Main street and up to Amador, where we turned east. We drove to Church and turned north and went about a half-block. We parked near the bowling alley [corner of Church and Bowman] to watch a man we saw hanging around Cactus Liquor store up the street, and to watch for the man following Miss Coogler.
>
> Then Miss Coogler came around the corner by Gateway Gardens and came down Church street. While we were watching the two men up the street, and watching her walk along the sidewalk, a car came slowly down Church street, going the same direction as Miss Coogler. It turned west on Bowman Street and stopped about 40 feet from the corner of Church and Bowman. We saw Miss Coogler leave the sidewalk and get in. We did not know which way it turned when it reached Main street.
>
> We did not follow the car because the patrol wagon would not start and because the man was still loitering near Cactus Liquor.

To my best recollection, the car Miss Coogler got into was a 1941 or 1942 Chevrolet coach. It was cream-yellow in color. . . .

There have been some rumors that the officers on duty that night know who was driving the car that picked up Miss Coogler, but I can state that if I knew who the person was, I would have reported to the authorities at once. (*LCSN*, May 13, 1949)

A *Sun-News* reporter had quoted the two policemen on April 20, 1949, as saying the car was light gray or light blue. An *El Paso Herald-Post* article on July 16, 1949, said "the policeman in one statement said the car was blue-green."

At Nuzum's trial, two years later, Officer Lucero had died, reportedly from a chronic ailment, so Reuben Flores alone testified again as to the time Cricket entered the car—specifically 3:25 a.m. on March 31. The testimony of anyone who said they saw Cricket after 3:00 a.m. was, of course, critical. Officer Flores said he was positive the car Cricket entered was not a maroon 1949 sedan like Nuzum's. He said, "Just to tell the truth, me and my partner, Lucero, didn't pay much attention to the car she got into. We often saw her walking along downtown Las Cruces streets late at night" (*EPHP*, April 9, 1951). Flores and Lucero were given truth serum (sodium pentothal) tests in El Paso during the grand jury investigation. Byron Darden, special prosecutor for the grand jury, said the truth serum tests were inconclusive. Both Lucero and Flores were cited by the Doña Ana County Grand Jury for drinking on duty, presumably on the night in question (*EPHP*, November 19, 1949).

Sylba Bryant, former border patrol officer, said that the two state policemen sent to investigate the case told him that Cricket had been seen about 3:00 a.m. knocking on the door of a bar on Church, most likely Barncastle's Gateway Gardens, which would have been closed by that time. A midblock alley afforded easy access to the rear door of that bar, or she could have knocked on the front door. The police also caused Bryant's heart to skip a beat when they told him they had "made" the car Cricket entered—a 1941 or 1942 two-tone Chevy—but they could not put a driver in it. Bryant owned one of only two such cars in the city. The other belonged to Gateway Gardens manager Freddy Barncastle. The officers told Bryant the suspect car was a coupe. Bryant's was a sedan. The coupe was Barncastle's (VI).

Another eyewitness downtown that morning was W. C. McBride, a Socorro rancher in Las Cruces to celebrate his birthday. He said he saw a light gray car with official state of New Mexico license plates (recognizable because of the number of digits, only three, without the customary additional county digits carried by all passenger and commercial vehicles), parked on the south side of May around 3:00 a.m. McBride said he was just getting out of a taxi on the corner of May and Church when he saw Cricket Coogler running on Church Street, often glancing behind her. If she knocked at Gateway Gardens, McBride should have observed this, but he did not mention it. McBride said he himself knocked on the door of Gateway Gardens, which was closed, and owner Freddy Barncastle, who obviously recognized him, let him in. McBride said he stayed inside only a few minutes, and when he came back, Cricket and the car were gone.

McBride did not explain why he stayed so briefly in Gateway Gardens. His description of a state license plate could serve to deflect suspicion from any local vehicle, especially one belonging to McBride's friend, Freddy Barncastle. McBride did identify the color of the car as gray, the same as Barncastle's.

District attorney T. K. Campbell commented that he found many things not feasible about W. C. McBride's testimony, particularly McBride's description of the car as a state car. Campbell did not explain why that or any other comment of McBride's was not credible. McBride reportedly said he felt Cricket's murder was an inside job, and one might assume he meant that law-enforcement officers had been involved.

Taking into consideration the lapse of time between 3:05, when the two Las Cruces officers saw Cricket on the corner of Main and Griggs, 3:10, when she was seen on May Street in front of the Western Union office, and 3:25, when she entered a car on Bowman, it appeared to district attorney T. K. Campbell that Cricket had waited on the corner of May and Church for several minutes. He told a local reporter he considered that pause apparent evidence that she had a rendezvous with someone at that point.

LaFel Oman was a prosecuting attorney hired, along with Byron Darden, by the Doña Ana County Grand Jury. In the video *The Silence of Cricket Coogler*, narrator John Ehrlichman quotes Oman as saying that Cricket Coogler had been partying with Santa Feans the night she disappeared. Two waitress friends of Cricket said that Cricket told them she and another girl friend had a double date with an officer and a politician from

Santa Fe on that night (*EPHP*, May 21, 1949). They supposedly named the men to the grand jurors in closed session. If Cricket did see an officer and a Santa Fean or two, it must have been before 9:30 p.m. or after 3:00 a.m., because the hours in between were pretty well accounted for in downtown cafés and the Del Rio Bar, in the company of Green Eyes Mosley and/or Jerry Nuzum.

If the district attorney was correct, Cricket may have had an appointment with someone who was not willing to come into the DeLuxe Café to pick her up—someone who expected her to be at a certain point that would take only a few seconds to exit. If the person(s) in that car was a well-known politician and/or a married local man, he might indeed have preferred a quieter street.

Mrs. J. R. Craddock, who lived at 241 East Griggs, next door to the VFW Club, said she heard a woman and two men arguing loudly almost in front of her home about 4:00 a.m. She said the woman was crying. She then heard the woman scream out, "I thought you were going to take me home." Mrs. Craddock said she heard a thud and then sudden silence. She ran to her window to try to see the car, but it drove off west (*EPHP*, May 31, 1949). Had it gone east, it would have passed her window. She could not help identify the car, but Mrs. Craddock may have overheard an abduction, or even—because of the sudden silence—a murder. How many crying women were out on the street in those few blocks of Las Cruces at that hour of that morning in the company of two men? And if Cricket got into a car initially at Bowman and Church, it moved immediately and could have been a couple of blocks north when she jumped out, within hearing distance of Mrs. Craddock. If burly Jerry Nuzum twice could not handle little Cricket Coogler outside the DeLuxe Café, perhaps it took two men to subdue her.

Cricket's physical state is an important element in her behavior that fateful evening. Current research recognizes the progressive effects of alcohol on the human body. A brief review of those effects, particularly on a body under a hundred pounds, sheds light on Cricket's condition:

Euphoria, Blood Alcohol Content (BAC) 0.03 to 0.12%—More self-confident, daring, attention span shortens, may look flushed, judgment not as good (expressing the first thought that comes to mind rather than an appropriate comment for the situation), trouble with fine movements. (Side effects: lowering of inhibitions, stimulation of the portions of the brain's cortex responsible for thinking and pleasure seeking) [Former boyfriend Lauren Welch told FBI agents Cricket was oversexed when she drank.]

Excitement, BAC 0.09 to 0.25%—Sleepy, trouble understanding, not reacting to situations as quickly (if they spill a drink, they may just stare at it), uncoordinated, losing balance easily, blurry vision. [Cricket's drink did spill, and she commented she would never live to wear those clothes again anyway.]

Confusion, BAC 0.18 to 0.30%—Profound confusion, uncertain where they are or what they are doing ["I thought you were taking me home," etc.], dizziness, staggering [Cricket fell while attempting to run], heightened emotional state—aggressive, withdrawn, or overly affectionate, sometimes nausea and vomiting.

Stupor, BAC 0.25 to 0.4%—Movement severely impaired, lapses in and out of consciousness, completely unaware of surroundings, actions, high risk of death.

Coma, BAC 0.35 to 0.50%—Unconsciousness, depressed reflexes, slow and shallow breathing, drop in heart rate, and usually death.

Death, BAC more than 0.50%—Failure of central nervous system. (Accessed February 25, 2006, at http://en.Wikipedia.org/wiki/Alcohol_poisoning)

Cricket had been drinking for more than six hours, and she was weary and emotional. She may have had an intensely personal reason for tears that night of March 30–31, 1949. She might have been pregnant, or feared that she was. Lauren Welch, who said he had been recently "going around with" her, told an FBI interviewer that Cricket had at some point gone to Florida (three aunts of Cricket lived in Florida) and given birth to twins, fathered by a former employee at the Tortugas. Cricket herself was a twin. A Las Cruces woman, Ethel J., alleged the following in a June 1, 1949, letter to district attorney T. K. Campbell, which he passed to attorney Byron Darden: "Whoever killed Cricket was . . . someone she knew. . . . She told several of her friends that she was going to have a baby, that Apodaca was the father, and that she had talked to him about her condition and wanted him to marry her but he told her that it would be impossible for him to marry her because he already had a wife and two or three children" (DP). Mr. Darden replied for Campbell and politely invited Mrs. J. to give testimony to the grand jury and/or inform him immediately as to who could confirm her information. No response from Mrs. J. was indicated.

In contrast, an acquaintance who had worked downtown in close proximity to Cricket Coogler stated that she did not recall Cricket's ever leaving town for any extended time, and that Cricket always had a job, was a good worker, and had never been fired (AI). But Cricket did leave the Tortugas, her favorite workplace, for some reason, and being fired is a plausible one.

Since Cricket Coogler was a favorite topic for gossip, stories about her possible pregnancies might be expected. Attitudes about things young girls just didn't do could be quite rigid in 1949, and the buzz around café and kitchen tables was full of stinging accusations.

If Cricket was, or ever had been, pregnant, and if she had even minimally threatened the father with some kind of blackmail, or the refusal of an abortion, that could have provided a possible motive for violence or murder.

Cricket's knowledge of gambling payoffs was another possible subject of blackmail, and another motive for someone to hurt her. People said she accompanied VIPs to El Paso more than once—with, of course, opportunity to observe them at any stops at gambling houses along the way. Cricket, in a moment of overconfidence, could have made the mistake of threatening a powerful man or talking too much about what she knew.

A note in the Darden Papers indicates two additional unsubstantiated stories that may have originated around a kitchen table. A telephone operator was supposed to have seen Happy Apodaca dancing with Cricket Coogler either the night before or night of Cricket's disappearance, and a maid at a local motel said the night before Cricket disappeared, she saw Happy Apodaca with her at the El Patio Bar in Old Mesilla.

Some people seemed willing to help Cricket Coogler the night she disappeared. Some were buying her coffee to sober her up; several were offering to take her home. Many moments of help, at least temporary help, were available to Cricket that evening; but she did not ask for any and accepted very little—a couple cups of coffee and some toast from Luther Mosley. She must have been mentally and physically exhausted as she was taken away in that dark morning from the downtown area of Las Cruces.

Far from rolling up its sidewalks early on that Wednesday night in March 1949, the town of Las Cruces was humming with a good many people long after midnight.

A most fascinating circumstance in the study of the Coogler case is that Cricket Coogler was last seen in the early morning hours of Thursday, March 31, 1949. By two o'clock that very afternoon, both Sheriff Happy Apodaca and football player Jerry Nuzum had driven 224 miles north to the city of Albuquerque. And if the reports of some were accurate, state corporation commissioner Dan Sedillo also traveled by car out of Las Cruces on March 31 toward his home and office in Santa Fe. The best road from Las Cruces to Santa Fe passed through Albuquerque. Albuquerque to Santa Fe was an hour's easy drive to the northeast.

5 The Body Is Found, Shoeless

Ollie Coogler, Cricket's mother, was frightened. If Cricket was not going to come home any evening, she was good about letting her mother know. Ollie waited throughout Thursday, March 31, and about eight o'clock Friday morning, April 1, she called the office she felt was appropriate—the office of Sheriff Happy Apodaca. She told him that Cricket was missing. Apodaca mentioned the possibility that Cricket had just run away, but assured Ollie that every lead would be investigated, and that so far there was no indication that the girl had met with foul play. Her mother described Cricket as eighteen years old, five feet two inches, about a hundred pounds, scar from a burn on left leg, gray suit, red shoes, red purse. She remembered to say Cricket had not taken her billfold that evening (*LCSN,* April 9, 1949).

It was a staggering five days before Sheriff Apodaca made public the fact that a local person was missing, and then on Wednesday, April 6, the *Las Cruces Sun-News* headline implied she had been missing only one day: "Pretty Cruces Girl Is Missing Since Tuesday." Tuesday would have been the previous day, April 5. Cricket had been missing since the previous Thursday, March 31. Regardless of the misstatement, there seemed to be a deliberately late start in the search for Cricket. It was April 9, 1949, before Sheriff Apodaca urged that anyone who could shed some light on her mysterious disappearance should contact the sheriff's office.

On April 12, 1949, after what must have been for Ollie Coogler an excruciating period of mounting fear, she asked Sheriff Apodaca to organize a posse to search for Cricket. The sheriff, feeling the additional pressure of front-page stories, phone calls, and assorted complaints, responded by recruiting thirty Boy Scouts to help in the search and announced he would lead them himself, beginning east of the city. The possible impact that finding a dead body could have on the young Scouts was not addressed, and it need not have been, since Cricket's remains lay twelve miles to the south.

On April 15, 1949, the day before Cricket's body was found, "Sid" Howard, who lived in nearby Mesilla Park, found a red shoe about four feet from the west side of Highway 80 while he was driving toward Mesquite, a village eight miles south of Las Cruces. He said he first saw the shoe about April 4, but did not pick it up until he read about what Cricket Coogler had been wearing the night of her disappearance. He also said he saw blue or green paint on the sole (*LCSN*, April 17, 1949; and *EPHP*, April 18 and May 11, 1949). He called Sheriff Apodaca and informed him of the find. Apodaca said he would get back in touch with him, and when he did, he simply asked Howard to "bring the shoe to Las Cruces the next time he came up" (DP).

Apodaca did take the shoe to the Electric Shoe Shop, where workmen identified a brace they had fitted against the heel for Cricket's sister. Under questioning at the Nuzum trial in 1951, Howard described changes that had been made in the shoe—a crack in the under sole, which had also been softened (*EPHP*, June 27, 1951), as if sandpapered.

The same day they received it, officers took the small red toeless pump, Cricket's right shoe, to Ollie Coogler, and she and Cricket's sister, Willow Rhea "Cookie" Bamert, identified it as one Cricket had been wearing. Handling that small shoe undoubtedly reduced their slim hopes that Cricket might still turn up unharmed.

The shoe caught the attention of reporter Alice Gruver, who went immediately to ask Sheriff Apodaca about it:

[His] responses were very peculiar. He just brushed me off, said that shoe "didn't amount to anything," when anyone knows it may have provided vital evidence in a murder case. (VI)

About four in the afternoon on April 16, the Saturday before Easter Sunday, 1949, four young rabbit hunters (two sets of brothers)—Jerry and Glenn Smith, 19 and 17, and Jerry and Charles Hawkins, 17 and 14—made a harrowing discovery in the desert near the Mesquite cemetery, about fifteen miles south of Las Cruces. Jerry Hawkins described the find to Walt Finley:

> We were hunting rabbits when Jerry Smith found the body. We looked at the body for a few minutes before walking back to the car. Then we drove to my house and called the officers.
>
> All four of us went to Carpenter's store to wait for the officers. When Deputy Sheriff Roy Sandman arrived, [we] all got into his car except my brother, Charles. He waited at the store.
>
> We showed Deputy Sheriff Sandman the body. The woman was lying on her back. Her clothes were pushed up around her neck. The lower portion of the body was naked. It looked like someone had put two or three shovels of sand on top of her.
>
> There were car tracks on the dirt road about 35 feet from the body. It looked like someone might have turned a car around after getting rid of the girl. When Sheriff Apodaca got here, I think he drove over the car tracks I had noticed. (*EPHP*, May 13, 1949)

The following words were attributed to Jerry Smith, but Jerry said he never spoke to reporters. So this version must have come from his brother Glenn or from one of the other boys, and the reporter credited Jerry Smith in error:

> I was running toward a rabbit when I first saw the body. I stopped and called the other boys over. We got in the car and drove to the Hawkins home and phoned the sheriff's office.
>
> When we went back to the grave, I saw some car tracks near the body. I don't know whether the tracks were deep enough to be of much help or not. The wind had been blowing for several days.
>
> When Sheriff Apodaca arrived, he drove his car over the tracks and on past the body, turned, and started back toward the body. In other words, he half circled the body with his car. He stopped the car about 30 or 40 feet from the body.
>
> He seemed nervous just like everybody else. He started swinging his arms. . . .
>
> Tommy Graham . . . told Happy he couldn't pick up the body in

the ambulance he was driving. He said he would have to go back to Las Cruces and get another ambulance. I rode with him back to my house. (*EPHP*, May 13, 1949)

In an in-person interview, Jerry Smith, who did indeed spot the body first, said not only that the quotes attributed to him were not his, but that he did not go with the others to Carpenter's Store, nor did he have any impression at the time that Sheriff Apodaca tried to obscure tracks. Jerry Smith decided to wait at the site of the body. The site would not otherwise have been easily relocated, because it lay in the midst of miles of desert dotted profusely with mesquite bushes three to five feet tall, growing densely among arroyos and patches of soft, loose sand.

Chilling details stayed in Jerry Smith's memory. He said Cricket's whole body was flattened, and her blackened toes and clawlike fingers were tipped with bright red nail polish (AI). She had no doubt intended to leave an impression wildly opposite from that terrible and indelible print in the mind of Jerry Smith.

Smith remembered that when Sheriff Apodaca arrived, he looked at the body, lifted her skirt, which was already pushed up above her knees, and said, "That's her all right" (AI). Another image with staying power is that of Sheriff Apodaca pacing at the site, swinging his arms—the sort of human behavior typical of extreme agitation.

There was a brief hullabaloo over whether car tracks were seen or not seen, but at least two of the rabbit hunters confirmed that they noticed no car or foot tracks visible near the body when they found it (*LCSN*, June 27, 1951). Anyone who has spent a few typical March or April windy days in southern New Mexico would not expect tracks in that area's sandy places to remain more than a few hours, sometimes minutes. So the question of tracks was swept away.

But a newspaper report of shovel marks found around the grave (*EPHP*, April 19, 1949) gave Cissy Lara's family pause. She remembers that her mother told of being at the kitchen sink in their Mesquite home the night Cricket disappeared, and seeing a car come around the corner from the road and circle their house without any lights. She of course thought it strange. The next morning, Cissy's father discovered a shovel missing. He never found it (AI).

Cricket's body was found a few hundred yards north of the Mesquite cemetery. Border patrolman Sylba Bryant said the killer must have known the area well, because at the time, the route to where her body was found involved turning off on a canal-bank road and curving down it about half a mile before turning west to where the body was dumped (VI). And there Cricket lay, close to a large, pale green mesquite bush, beneath a little cool sand, without her blue and gray plaid jacket, without panties, without shoes. She had been missing seventeen days.

April 17, 1949, Easter Sunday morning, the day after Cricket's body was found, M. O. Johnson reported that a few days earlier he had found another high-heeled red pump lying along Highway 80, as much as five hundred feet farther south from where the first shoe was found the previous Friday. Like Sid Howard, Johnson did not realize at first that the shoe could be important evidence in a murder case. He said he placed a brick at the spot he found the shoe, then hung it in a tree in front of his home, perhaps thinking the owner might retrace steps and spot it (*EPHP*, May 14, 1949). There it had hung during an intensive nighttime search on Saturday, April 16.

The Saturday-night search was conducted by four young Las Cruces men: Jess Williams Jr., Francis Bennett, Billy Durio, and Frank Brownfield. Driving slowly along the edge of Highway 80, using the headlights as well as flashlights, they searched in both directions from where the first shoe had been found. They found things such as cigarette butts, beer cans, matchbook covers, but no shoe or other clue. There was very little foliage and the land was pretty level. When they read that the second shoe had been found, they were convinced they would have seen the second shoe if it had been where Johnson reportedly found it, and that the shoe had been planted sometime between 11:00 p.m. Saturday night and the time it was found on Sunday.

M. O. Johnson explained that as soon as he became aware of the shoe's possible significance, he called Sheriff Apodaca at a very early hour. Johnson told the sheriff that he thought he had Cricket's other shoe. Apodaca responded briefly and hung up. About fifteen minutes later, Apodaca called Johnson back. "What did you say to me earlier this morning?" he asked. Johnson repeated his message and Apodaca drove out to pick up the shoe (*LCSN*, May 14, 1949). Johnson's explanation seemed to puncture the theory that the second shoe had been planted.

The eerie placement of the two shoes, several hundred feet apart, gave range to all kinds of speculation about how the shoes came off Cricket's feet and why they landed so far apart: she jumped or fell from the car; she was run over by a car that caught one shoe temporarily; one shoe was lost in dragging her along the road, the other tossed out a car window; the shoes came off as she ran; and so forth.

Ollie Coogler no doubt had visualized all of those possibilities once the shoes were located. Whoever had the difficult task of telling Mrs. Coogler that her daughter's body had been found will likely never forget the moment. She must have backed away, physically and mentally, from the news she had suspected and feared. She later said:

I don't know who would want to kill my daughter.

If we could find a blue-gray plaid coat, an ox-blood bag, or the panties my baby was wearing the night she was killed, we might be able to solve this murder.

When I reported my daughter missing to Sheriff Apodaca on April 1, after searching for her two days, he told me Ovida had ran [*sic*] away from home.

After I identified a red shoe found by Sid Howard, . . . the sheriff thought I didn't know what I was talking about. I haven't talked to him since.

Even after my daughter's body was found, the sheriff never did talk with me. District Attorney Tommy Campbell never has spoken to me. Neither one has bothered to tell me if any evidence has been uncovered in the case.

Several of my friends have told me I had better be quiet and not push the investigation if I knew what is good for me. But when you have a daughter murdered, you feel like you have to do something. (*EPHP*, May 7, 1949)

It sounds incredible that neither the sheriff nor the district attorney spoke to Mrs. Coogler after Cricket's body was found, either to obtain vital information or even as a courtesy. It was as if Cricket's family became invisible to some. Nevertheless, Cricket's brother Willie told Finley, "I don't have much to work with . . . but no one is going to scare me. I'll never rest until the killer gets what he deserves" (*EPHP*, May 7, 1949).

On May 5, 1949, Hubert Beasley, described by a diplomatic Governor Thomas Mabry as the best police chief the state had ever had, dispatched two of his men, Captain Ben Martinez and Officer Nolan Utz, to Las Cruces to investigate Cricket Coogler's death. Chief Beasley, a native of Tennessee, was a tall, lanky cowboy type, attractive, but with the look of a man with little humor. Hubert Beasley was to find less and less to smile about in the early 1950s. He became more and more involved in the investigation, inserting himself into one of the ugliest aspects of the Coogler case, and soon enough had reason to regret it.

6   The Body Handlers

By the time the rabbit hunters notified the sheriff's office and led investigators and a Graham's Mortuary hearse to the site, it was after dark on April 16, 1949. The group had to wait while Tommy Graham drove the hearse back to Las Cruces and arranged for a local florist to take a flower delivery truck out to pick up the decomposing body and deliver it to the elegant, newly constructed Graham's Mortuary for examination. In the absence of today's array of plastics, a body bag of waxed canvas was likely used, and a mess in an expensive hearse was saved.

The examination of Cricket's body did not follow usual procedure. Gleaning any truth from that body may have been beyond the science of the day, but the effort that went into the task seemed halfhearted. When found, Cricket's body was wearing only a skirt, brassiere, and blouse. Apodaca confirmed that the panties, shoes, stockings, and suit jacket were missing.

Tommy Graham, part owner of the mortuary, described the condition of Cricket's body when he arrived at the makeshift grave in Mesquite about 7:30 p.m. He said A. L. Apodaca, Roy Sandman, and Max Johnson (perhaps the same Johnson who had found one of Cricket's shoes) were present, and that Apodaca's car was within thirty-five feet of the body. He said her face was skinned, the body lying face up with arms at the sides and legs straight out, and her skirt was above her knees, but no clothes were torn. Graham confirmed that no examination was made to determine whether she had been the victim of a sex attack since the body was so decomposed.

However, he said an examination did show that her left collarbone had been broken and there seemed to be a skull fracture above the left ear (*EPHP*, May 12, 1951).

Graham, who had known Cricket for about eight years, also noted that her face, arms, and legs were cut and bruised, and that she appeared to have received "quite a blow" over her left eye (*EPHP*, June 27, 1951).

A twelve-man coroner's jury was hastily summoned. Dr. Dan Maddox was asked to examine the decomposed body. Years later, on videotape, Maddox said that the jury stayed only a moment, exiting the mortuary's examining room quickly because of the odor. Then as now, coroner's juries often were pro forma affairs, usually resulting in an endorsement of the coroner's findings. Dr. Dan Maddox:

> I was in the hospital and got a call from Graham's Mortuary.... [The body] had been identified as Cricket Coogler by friends or family before I arrived. We were a small town and I was the only surgeon. There was no pathologist, and autopsies had to be performed in El Paso.... Sending the body to El Paso for an autopsy was discussed, but I advised that it was unnecessary, because although an autopsy could describe where internal organs had been moved, the body was so thoroughly crushed that it could not be more specific than my own examination.... She was so slim and her skin so moveable that I could easily describe fractures by simply feeling. And her chest, abdomen, shoulder, and internal organs were so crushed and she was so torn up, it was clear she died of massive and severe trauma. ... I was told she was an indigent and therefore could not afford to have that [an autopsy] done. (VI)

If the Coogler family were ever approached with the question of autopsy costs, it would seem most inappropriate, since a possible murder had occurred and the county should have paid for transporting the body for autopsy as a part of its investigation—not to mention the insult of labeling the hardworking Coogler family "indigent."

Maddox's initial description also said that the right side of her face had been smashed with a blunt object, her left collarbone was broken, and dark bruises marked the flesh inside her right thigh. But later he reversed his opinion and said the body was too decomposed to determine something like bruises. Another possibility is that what looked like bruises were areas in various degrees of decomposition.

Yet another of Dr. Maddox's official statements was that "there were no skinned or lacerated places on her body, as there would be if she fell, jumped, was shoved from a car, or was run over" (*LCSN*, May 9, 1949). Then, again refuting himself years later on videotape, Maddox surmised that Cricket might well have been run over multiple times by an automobile, the path of smashed bones and organs being too close together to have been crushed in only one pass. Significantly, the X-rays did not show very many broken bones, despite Maddox's use of the word "crushed." Forensic anthropologist Dave Weaver proposed that in sixteen days of exposure and decomposition, the chest could have collapsed and scavengers could have destroyed and even moved internal organs or what remained of them. Weaver suggested the possibility that all the damage to the body, including the eye out of the socket and the skinned face, could easily have happened postmortem, although any facial injuries could have accelerated postmortem changes in those injured areas. Weaver also said that even the fractured left collarbone "might have been a postmortem effect, considering that scavenging carnivores sometime chew through or break bones like the clavicle, which are relatively small and underlie points at which they might try to open or move a body" (AI). However, one common injury sustained in a fall from a moving car or a pickup bed is a broken collarbone.

Maddox did not disguise his disdain of Cricket Coogler. He called her a "bar fly" and described her in the company of politicians a couple of weeks before her death:

> Apparently she was very active that weekend. . . . She was in the middle of the saloon and drinking with everybody. . . . Apparently they spent three or four hours, [Cricket] sitting in the laps of all of them. She would go out for a while and come back in. Nobody really knew. . . . Everyone there was suspicious of everyone else because all of them had been with her that evening. (VI)

Underlying dismissive attitudes toward Cricket, such as Maddox's, may partially explain why evidence from her body was not more carefully preserved, why her family was not more respectfully treated, and why facts would be hidden to protect lives deemed much more "important" than

Cricket's. Such disdain made it easier to shrug off the importance of evidence that certainly was within reach for only a short window of time.

Counter to usual practice, a local reporter was in attendance at the initial examination of the body, and he was critical of the process:

> No samples of deposits under her fingernails were taken. Her clothing was not removed or examined for evidence of a sex crime . . . [and] the coroner's jury did not view the body. It was being placed in the casket when they entered the room. The examining physician related to them what he had found and then they filed out.
>
> An unquotable sheriff's office source disclosed that no pictures were taken at the scene of the shallow grave. (*LCSN*, May 8, 1949)

No one took a camera to the desert gravesite.

On the Monday morning after the body was discovered, Sheriff Apodaca made a statement to the press, whether a guess or an inadvertent revelation, that Cricket Coogler had been the victim of a brutal sex attack. Dr. Maddox, on videotape years later, appeared to agree with Apodaca: "I'm sure rape occurred. Her pelvis was fractured also." However, an examination of the disinterred body by another physician revealed no fracture of the pelvis. Pelvic bones separate during decomposition, and this is more likely with no underwear to hold things in place. The absence of panties alone signals a sexual element, consensual or not. Some of Dr. Maddox's observations might have been essentially correct, but his explanations wrong (Weaver).

Then there was the matter of the powdered lime poured over the body of Cricket Coogler in her casket. Undertaker Tommy Graham explained that when the body was first prepared for burial, over a hundred pounds of lime were placed over it to kill the odor (as well as larvae). Dr. Maddox said that lime had been his suggestion, in order to enable the family to hold services in the presence of that decomposing body if that was their wish (VI). Quicklime was likely used, since it is very corrosive, being highly alkaline. A body already in advanced decomposition would have been very susceptible to the effects of lime (Weaver). At any rate, Cricket's body could not have been normally embalmed, and so the lime treatment seemed justifiable.

Cricket's family opted for quiet graveside services at the Masonic Cemetery on the morning of April 18, 1949. Ovida was survived by her mother; a twin brother, William; and two sisters: Mrs. Carl Bamert ("Cookie") of Muleshoe, Texas, and Mrs. V. L. Meadows (Varela) of Baytown, Texas. Cookie was said to resemble her sister Cricket.

Ten days after the cemetery service, State Chief of Police Hubert Beasley arrived in Las Cruces. His office first explained that he was on a routine inspection trip of southern New Mexico state police officers, but he was immediately involved in investigating the Coogler case, prompting speculation that some high Santa Fe official might have sent him to help Happy Apodaca accomplish a quick and thorough blockage of any investigative trails leading to the state government offices in Santa Fe.

Beasley insisted that he wanted Cricket's body exhumed to look for skid marks or tire marks to determine whether she had been run over. Dr. Maddox had a little confrontation with Chief Beasley about the futility of exhumation. "I reminded him she was buried in lime but he insisted," recalled Maddox on videotape. "There [would be] no skin on which to search for tire marks. . . . I asked him [again] later and then thought I'd better get out of there because he was pretty irate."

Tommy Graham also pronounced that exhuming the body would prove useless. "What do they expect to find?" he asked. "The murderer's name engraved on one of the bones?" (*EPHP*, May 7, 1949).

If Maddox and Graham sounded a bit offended by the idea of exhumation, they likely felt their professional work and opinions were being questioned. Forensic expert Dave Weaver: "In the medico-legal climate of the times, exhumation sometimes was taken as a slap in the face of the examiner, rather like getting a second opinion concerning surgery."

Judge W. T. Scoggin Jr. signed a court order for disinterring Cricket's body on the afternoon of May 5, 1949. Exhumation took place around noon on May 7, and the inquest was held again at Graham's Mortuary. Again, a few oddities were reported:

> The public health office, contrary to custom, was not notified of the disinterrment [*sic*]. An X-ray technician . . . was not there by order of a physician, despite the fact that such an order is required.
>
> The examination was conducted under a cloak of secrecy.
>
> Milo Sherwood, an attendant at the mortuary, . . . had strict orders from officers to admit no one and to release no information. A *Sun-News* reporter who tried to gain admittance overheard a man say, "If he comes in here, we'll shoot the s.o.b." (*LCSN*, May 9, 1949)

After the criticisms published by the reporter who was present at the first examination, there was understandable double caution about prohibiting reporters the second time.

Cricket's body was returned to its grave about four in the afternoon of the same day. Information about this second examination was hard to come by. Dr. Leland Evans examined the body. The lime, sure enough, had left only a skeleton. His official report confirmed a fracture line on the left temple, fractured cheek and jaw bones, as well as a complete break in the left collarbone. He found no evidence of fracture in the legs or pelvis. Dr. Evans also said Cricket might have died of a broken neck, because the X-ray showed a shattered vertebra at the point where the neck joins the body. However, because of the lime, interpretation of the films could not be adhered to strictly. In 2005 specialist Dave Weaver confirmed that lime contains a lot of calcium, which can absorb radiation and therefore blur an X-ray.

The verdict of the first coroner's jury at the inquest on April 16 was "death from an unknown object or person." But after the exhumation, wording on Cricket's death certificate was changed slightly to "death of a violent nature by an unknown (homicide, suicide or accident) cause" (*LCSN*, May 9, 1949). Even if examination rules had been followed to the letter, this was perhaps as close as anyone could come to a conclusion at the time.

Contrary to today's procedures, there was no routine examination to determine pregnancy, past or present, and it is likely that no thought was given to that contingency by examiners. Even if it had been considered, given the condition of the body, an early pregnancy would have been difficult to identify.

The bottom line: It simply was not established whether Cricket Coogler had been murdered or not, run over or not, pregnant or not, sexually assaulted or not.

Dr. Dan Maddox displayed a little smile on videotape as he said, "The Grand Jury asked me if I thought it had been a murder, and I said it would have been hard for her to do that much damage to herself." Murder was not proven by the evidence, but neither could murder be excluded by the evidence.

No one could say March 30–31, 1949, was actually the night Cricket died. That was simply the last night several people saw her, and so it seemed a reasonable assumption. However, an inspector at the New Mexico Port of Entry near Anthony, New Mexico—Robert Estrada—said he saw a girl he believed was Cricket Coogler shortly after midnight on April 1 on the highway, about twenty hours after Cricket was last seen in Las Cruces. He said he was driving south on Highway 80 on his way to his Anthony home (about twenty-five miles south of Las Cruces) after work when he saw a girl, dressed in a sort of gray suit, running along the highway. He said she was running unsteadily, as if somewhat drunk or wobbly, on high-heel shoes, and she was calling for help. He began a U-turn when a dark green Chevrolet or International pickup truck came by, heading north. He said the pickup stopped and two men got out. One began beating the girl; then the girl was thrown into the truck and it sped north again. Estrada said he thought at the time it was some kind of early morning family fight, but after he read about Cricket Coogler in the news, he left word at Sheriff Apodaca's home that he had some important information in the Coogler case. Estrada said no one ever contacted him about his report (*EPHP*, May 19, 1949). Here was another vehicle to be added to the already long list of different colors, makes, and models under suspicion. It would have been an important story to examine, since a one-day delay in Cricket's death could threaten some alibis, strengthen others.

Cricket's body yielded few clues about the cause of her death, and Las Crucens became fed up with the lack of progress in the case. Most of the city was embarrassed and saddened about the horror one of their own young women had endured. Some muttered about the treatment of her remains. There were, of course, those few who knew much, said nothing, and had no complaints about the way the case was being handled.

7 The Doña Ana County Grand Jury

Citizens in the area had been patient at first when investigations in the Cricket Coogler case seemed to be proceeding fairly normally, according to the newspapers they followed daily. Walgreen's Drug Store, in an odd attempt to lighten spirits, offered on its luncheon menu a "Grand Jury Plate." Customers were to "subpoena" dishes by their temporary new names: "Indicted Salad Bowl," "Change of Venue Cheese," "Padlocked Tomato," "Handcuffed Ritz Crackers," and a macabre "Murdered Baked Ham" (*EPT*, August 12, 1949).

Asked to comment about the possible involvement of state officials, Governor Thomas Mabry announced that the case would not be whitewashed. He expressed his belief that state police chief Hubert Beasley was thoroughly qualified to handle the matter, and said the case would be explored from every angle in a thorough investigation. No suspect's name yet appeared in the news, just statements that Sheriff Apodaca had brought in five men for questioning—two from Las Cruces, one from Oklahoma, one from Kansas, and one from the Lower Mesilla Valley. A former Taxi Number Nine driver, Thomas York, was retrieved from Salt Lake City simply for questioning about an $8.50 cab fare from the DeLuxe Café to White Sands Proving Grounds at 2:25 a.m. on March 31, 1949. York checked back into the stand at 4:10 a.m. (*EPHP*, July 21, 1949). The Lower Mesilla Valley resident was likely Robert Templeton, a friend of Nuzum's; he was temporarily held for questioning and released (*EPHP*, July 19 and 23, 1949).

It is noteworthy that so many of the men sought for questioning had to be retrieved from other states only a few weeks following Cricket Coogler's death.

The *Las Cruces Sun-News*, tired of being scooped by Walt Finley at the *El Paso Herald-Post*, issued a front-page article May 6, 1949—"Sun-News Scooped As It Keeps Confidences"—claiming that the *Sun-News* knew about many details of the case but did not print those things in a conscientious effort to aid law enforcement. In an adjoining column, in what seemed an effort to prove they too could be tough, this Q and A exchange with district attorney T. K. Campbell appeared:

Reporter: Do you have a car besides Nuzum's impounded?
TKC: No comment.
Reporter: Have you questioned the doctor who examined the body?
TKC: No comment.
Reporter: Was the man you held on another charge [most likely
    Wesley Byrd] released for lack of evidence?
TKC: Let's not bring him into it now.

The ability to ask tough questions had to be the point of the story, because the answers certainly were not.

Walt Finley was a finalist for the Pulitzer Prize for his reporting of the Cricket Coogler case and surrounding stories. (The predictable winner that year had written about the history of the *New York Times*.) Finley's coverage of the case was hands-down the most thorough and most reliable. Finley said he began to cover the Coogler murder when his editor, Mike Michaels, asked him to catch a bus on his day off (Finley did not have a car at the time), go up to Las Cruces, and check on rumors about Sheriff Apodaca.

Finley initially spoke to Lloyd Hufstedler, the dry cleaner who said he had cleaned blood from Cricket Coogler's clothing on more than one occasion, and some other people in downtown Las Cruces, most of whom Walt said seemed fearful, afraid to say anything, often passing the buck to others. He said he stopped by J.C. Penney on Main Street to interview Ollie Coogler, Cricket's mother. Ollie told him Cricket had been "socially connected" with Happy Apodaca, and that the sheriff had brought Cricket home on several occasions. Finley said he could see how reluctant, even frightened, Ollie appeared. It was the same fear one could feel on the streets. But as he began publishing information from his interviews, a few more people began to speak up (VI).

The whole town was grousing, then complaining openly about the apparent stalling of the case. Attorney and former FBI agent Jess Weir made a statement to FBI investigators that

> The citizens of Las Cruces . . . had lost all confidence in the law enforcement officers in the town as well as the District Attorney. . . . At least 25 individuals, knowing [me] to be a former FBI agent, had . . . asked if there was any way that the Bureau could be brought into [the] investigation, inasmuch as they were disgusted with the way that it had been handled by Sheriff Apodaca and his assistants to date. (NARA3)

Cricket's brother-in-law, Carl Bamert, told the *Sun-News* that very early on, he had given Sheriff Apodaca the names of these three possible suspects, all of whom were eventually questioned by the grand jury and released: Jerry Nuzum, Luther Mosley, and Lauren Welch. Bamert complained that three days after he gave the sheriff Mosley's location in the town of Hot Springs, no efforts had been made to contact Mosley. Mosley himself later confirmed that Apodaca made no effort to question him. Carl Bamert also reported that he had located a car fitting a description of the one Cricket entered early on March 31, and that he gave all his information to Sheriff Apodaca, with no result.

Walt Finley's May 7, 1949, headline, "I Was the Fall Guy," referring to the arrest of football star Jerry Nuzum, who had yet to be charged with any crime, caused an uproar among local college students, and about three hundred of them attended a mass meeting held in the college football stadium to protest injustices in the handling of the Coogler case. Students and townspeople circulated a petition, signed by the required number of seventy-five people, calling for a grand jury investigation. The petition was presented to Judge W. T. Scoggin Jr. (proud to be one of the last New Mexicans to take and pass the bar exam without having attended law school, according to the *Las Cruces Bulletin*'s compiled pictorial history of the town). The legality of the petition was questioned at first, when it was feared that signers at the college would not qualify as resident tax payers.

However, the petition soon had a hundred legitimate signatures and was presented to Judge Scoggin. Scoggin announced that he would first have to ascertain whether funds were available to finance a grand jury probe. His check must have indicated adequate funds, and perhaps uncovered some testy tempers, because he quickly selected a jury of twelve. But the jury was not charged with finding a killer. District attorney T. K. Campbell explained that although a specific charge normally would be necessary to justify a grand jury, it was expected that this jury would try to find out whether authorities were lax in an attempt to catch Cricket's slayer, or whether any important evidence had been overlooked. Put another way, the Doña Ana County Grand Jury's formal mission was not to find a solution to the murder case or even to determine whether Cricket's death was a murder, only to investigate the manner in which the case had been handled. Nevertheless, Campbell and Byron Darden (local attorney appointed by Judge Scoggin to aid the DA) reassured people that the grand jury still had broad powers to explore all angles, including circumstances surrounding the Coogler death, reports of gambling in Doña Ana County, and three previous attacks on women in Las Cruces (two teenagers and a Canadian woman, all of whom named Happy Apodaca in assault allegations).

Names and testimony of grand jury witnesses were normally kept secret, with any disclosing person facing contempt, fine, or imprisonment. This grand jury included men from many walks of life. Whoever was responsible for Cricket Coogler's death, and whoever helped cover up evidence, probably did not expect much from this group of men. They were wrong.

THE MEMBERS OF THE DOÑA ANA COUNTY GRAND JURY:
- Hal R. Cox, foreman of the jury, prominent ranch owner
- Carroll Angus Boggs, Salem merchant (village of Salem is north of Las Cruces)
- James F. "Jim" Vermillion, Las Cruces barber
- Charles E. Neff Jr., Las Cruces tourist-court operator
- Allen Russell Soper, Hatch hotel operator
- Henry Melendres, Las Cruces grocer
- George W. Hay, Las Cruces farm equipment store manager
- Parker F. Davenport, El Paso Electric Company (Las Cruces manager)
- Joe E. Jones, radio technician

- R. A. Durio Jr., automobile mechanic
- Robert C. Garcia, bar manager in village of Doña Ana
- Edwin O. Kull, farmer

Esther Smith was the stenographer for the grand jury.

The first weeks of grand jury meetings did not go well, according to videotaped interviews with reporter Alice Gruver and jury members R. A. Durio and Russell Soper. Gruver said that district attorney T. K. Campbell "could not seem to [collect himself to] prosecute before the grand jury. His tongue would get twisted, etc." R. A. Durio (who incidentally went to school with Happy Apodaca and had always liked him) said the opening weeks were squandered on

a lot of foolishness. . . . When it takes two weeks to establish that the body was found in a certain spot, on and on with a lot of nothing, you are getting nowhere. So we hired two attorneys and then we got started. But all we could do was to piece odds and ends together. The Grand Jury was a mix of lots of different kinds of people—kind of like the army—you had no choice but to work with them. We met in the Court House. Cox was foreman, the most knowledgeable about how to run such a thing. . . . The most important accomplishment of the Grand Jury [was] cutting down on the vice in the state. It was bad. Very disappointing however that we didn't accomplish the primary job of finding out what happened to the girl.

There was a complete cover-up. . . . There were people inter-viewed who knew who the murderer was. . . . But if you can't get at the truth, then you can't. You can get some of them under oath and they will still lie to you. . . . I think it [Cricket's death] could have been accidental. (VI)

As to the statements of politicians interviewed, Durio said, "You know a politician can talk to you for thirty minutes and not say a word" (VI). Grand jury member Russell Soper said there was a tremendous reluctance of county employees to respond to questions, and he thought their few answers seemed coached (VI).

The Doña Ana County Grand Jury quizzed Jerry Nuzum extensively, as well as many others who had a version of Cricket's movements the night she disappeared. They spoke to city and county officials, people downtown that night, friends and co-workers of Cricket. But almost every statement was contradicted by other statements. The jury was getting nowhere.

The jury did subpoena the records of Happy Apodaca's bank account, which, at least to Russell Soper, certainly appeared to suggest some kind of payoffs, since they showed deposits of several lump sums that were multiples of his salary. For example, the notes of grand jury member R. A. Durio indicated routine deposits into Apodaca's account between $30 and $60; then suddenly, in February 1949, a deposit of $434 showed up. In March, a deposit of $388 was listed (AI). Happy may not have been asked to explain his bank account, but the jury at least noted those numbers.

In regard to responsibility for the death of Cricket Coogler, Russell Soper commented with painstaking deliberation: "Some heavy politicians were involved to the extent they tried to cover it up and they did a very, very good job" (VI).

Early on, the Doña Ana Grand Jury took two courageous, unusual, and unprecedented steps. As witnesses began talking about Cricket's acquaintances from Santa Fe and her possible knowledge about gambling payoffs, the grand jury became convinced it could take effective action against illegal gambling in the county. On June 23, 1949, armed with search warrants, the grand jury conducted its own raids of La Loma del Rey Club (Frank Ardovino's place), the Valley Country Club (Robert Milkman and Salvador Ardovino), the Sunland Club (Barney Marcus), and the Anthony Country Club (C. E. Dahlquist). One member of the grand jury accompanied each team of police, and the raids simultaneously struck at ten o'clock in the evening.

Prior to the grand jury's raids, police had attempted to raid these establishments, but by the time they got down south, as jury member R. A. Durio wryly put it, "everything was cleaned up and they were runnin' church in there" (VI). Someone was tipping off the owners in advance. On June 12, 1949, Judge Scoggin had ordered Sheriff Apodaca to raid the Las Cruces Elks Club, the VFW, and the Las Cruces Country Club, each of which had only a machine or two and some card-game gambling. But an FBI report noted that Scoggin had been completely bypassed by the grand jury on the large-scale June 23 raids, and comments from a confidential informant to the FBI (called "T-1") supported suspicions that Scoggin had been the leak for certain former raids:

Santos Ramirez [when he served as sheriff, preceding Happy Apodaca] had also had difficulty raiding gambling establishments due to a leak. Ramirez advised the informant that he was of the opinion that William T. Scoggin, Jr. [district attorney at the time] was responsible for leaks as to anticipated raids. (NARA3)

Apparently Judge Scoggin, whose lame leg required the use of a cane and who reportedly kept a small carafe of liquor, not water, at his courtroom bench, was also viewed with suspicion by Albert Clancy, assistant United States attorney. In an August 1950 letter to Ben Brooks in the U.S. Attorney General's Office in Washington, Clancy said: "Mr. Darden and I, after a full discussion of the matter, decided it might be better to stay away from Judge Scoggin, who incidentally was . . . out of Las Cruces to be gone another week or ten days" (NARA).

State supreme court justice J. C. Compton ordered three of the raided clubs closed until their owners could satisfy the court that they would not be used for illegal purposes. Frank Ardovino (La Loma del Rey) was found guilty of possessing and operating gambling equipment, fined $1,000, and sentenced to five months in the county jail. Robert Milkman (Valley Country Club) was found not guilty. Barney Marcus (Sunland Club or Tropics) was found guilty and fined $500 plus costs.

R. A. Durio had himself observed what he felt sure had been gambling-club payoffs: "A lot of us had seen politicians exchanging envelopes and you could kind of figure why. I remember one time I was in Billy Crews [restaurant] in El Paso and there was one of the big shots from Las Cruces. A guy passed him an envelope. He looked in it and put it in his pocket. Of course I couldn't see what was in it" (VI).

Raids by the dozens on statewide gambling establishments were soon reported. A former New Mexico secretary of state, Cecilia Tafoya Poarch, sister to state policeman Tuffy Tafoya, was arrested on April 18, 1950, as her Buckhorn Bar, in a neighboring county, was raided. Tuffy was reportedly part owner of the bar.

Some gambling joints had been enjoying additional special privileges.

The Darden Papers reveal that a couple of the beleaguered establishments in Anapra, the Valley Country Club and the Sunland Club, had enjoyed water privileges from a well owned by Anapra's justice of the peace, T. V. Garcia. Residents of Anapra who depended on water from that well sometimes had to wait two or three days for water, while the clubs were served first.

During the rash of gambling trials, it came to light that the Valley Country Club sported an interesting door disguised by a mirror, which concealed the entrance to a room with gambling equipment. Other sleights of hand are obvious in the following exchange between attorney Wayne Whatley (T. K. Campbell's law partner) and Barney Marcus of the Sunland Club:

> Whatley: How about the dice?
> Marcus: Oh, they were just old, beat-up dice we kept for people who wanted to make lamps out of them.
> Whatley: And the roulette table?
> Marcus: It wasn't a roulette table. Just part of one we kept in a little 3×5 liquor storeroom left over from previous raids.
> Whatley: And I suppose that those two brand-new slot machines, with money in them, were used by you as a savings bank?
> Marcus: Those slot machines were just for my own amusement and use. I got them for various organizations I belong to. (*EPHP*, July 15, 1949)

Marcus also contended that the Sunland Club, so named in the injunction, did not exist and was really "The Tropics." The big sign out front that read "Sunland Club" was not meaningful, Marcus contended, because another sign, "The Tropics," was posted inside the building. Whatley also asked state patrolman I. E. "Sally" Salazar, "Did Marcus tell you that the boys on the beat were entitled to be taken care of and that he proposed to see that you were taken care of?" Salazar answered, "Yes" (*EPHP*, July 15, 1949).

After several sessions, the Doña Ana County Grand Jury made a second, rather astonishing move, which commanded the attention of federal investigators as well as writers from *Time* magazine and the *New York Times*. The jury barred the judge, W. T. Scoggin Jr., and the district attorney, T. K. Campbell, from its proceedings. Then they hired attorneys Byron Darden and LaFel Oman and finally began producing indictments, making recommendations, and calling an important Santa Fean to come before them.

A buzz was created when state corporation commissioner Dan Sedillo appeared before the grand jury, where he read a statement but did not answer a single question. Russell Soper remembered Sedillo's appearance that day as nervous and apprehensive, which suggested to him some kind of guilt. Although his name was mentioned, Lt. Governor Joseph Montoya was not asked to account to the grand jury for his whereabouts on March 30–31, 1949, nor to respond to the stories that his office had checked out a state vehicle for that time (Hillerman, VI), nor whether the report that Montoya owned a half interest in one of the clubs in Anapra (Sylba Bryant, VI) was true.

As it closed its deliberations, the Doña Ana County Grand Jury pled for a judge from outside the Third Judicial District before making its report, thereby refusing to submit a report to Judge Scoggin. Supreme court chief justice Charles R. Brice sent one of his justices, James McGhee, from Santa Fe to receive the jury's report. Judge Brice may have overstepped a constitutional line in replacing Judge Scoggin with Judge McGhee, but Brice had been instrumental in writing the state's constitution, and no one challenged his decision. Judge James McGhee did receive a phone call saying that if he went to Doña Ana County, he'd go home in a casket (Ehrlichman, video narrator). He went anyway, and his presence instantly brought results.

McGhee arrived in Las Cruces on June 23, and the very next day, Sheriff Apodaca was indicted on ten counts, including gambling at the Las Cruces Country Club and Elks Club, permitting gambling at Valley Country Club, adultery, failure to account for money coming into his hands as sheriff, demanding and receiving illegal fees, drinking on duty while transporting a suspect, gross immorality in the attempted seduction of a minor at the home of Joe De Turo (see chapter 9), as well as gross incompetence and negligence in the following matters:

1. Allowing M. E. ("Loco") Garcia, county commission chairman, to enter the cell of Rosa P., a former Welcome Inn barmaid, and leaving them alone for about thirty minutes. [Rosa P. alleged that at that time Garcia beat her after her refusal of a date with him.]
2. Physically abusing [Coogler murder suspect] Wesley Byrd.
3. Making no move to investigate gambling at the Palms Liquor Store until 10:00 p.m., although he was notified of gambling in progress at 4:30 p.m.

4. Allowing justice of the peace Ramon Duran to maintain an office in the sheriff's office.
5. Removal of the contents of three jackpots from slot machines from the Mountain View Inn, which had been stored in the sheriff's office.
6. Delivery of two slot machines to a person for use as gambling devices.
7. Appointing V. D. Yelton a special deputy in spite of the fact that Yelton had been discharged as a game warden for conduct prejudicial to the United States and was currently under investigation.
8. Failure to take steps to protect possible evidence at the scene of Cricket Coogler's hasty initial burial.
9. Failing to contact ["Mr. Green Eyes"] Luther Mosley regarding the Coogler case.
10. Locking visitors to the jail [Mary Nuzum and landlady Eloise Ellis] in a cell for a short time.
11. (a) Grossly inadequate record keeping in the Coogler case [2004 Sheriff Juan Hernandez confirmed to the author that the file should have contained, for example, incident reports, pictures, statements, and disposition reports], and (b) failure to search the area where Cricket's shoe[s] were found.
12. Grossly inadequate records of the New Mexico A&M robbery case (in which $11,804 was stolen from a safe in the college business office in Hadley Hall).
13. Thirty-day delinquency in the records of the county jail.
14. Delayed cleanup of the jail and refusal to take federal prisoners in the jail.
15. Failing to keep facilities in the jail in good repair.
16. Ordering deputies to desist from enforcing gambling laws.
17. Failing to take any steps toward locating Cricket Coogler in the days immediately following her disappearance.
18. Improper mileage reports.
19. Ordering steaks, butter, and eggs for the jail, not intended for prisoners, for which the county was billed.
20. Failure to seize seventeen slot-machine stands at the Valley Country Club when the machines themselves were seized. [The reason here is obscure. Perhaps some important mechanism was located in the stand.]

21. Failure to take action as Roy Sandman reported gambling equipment in the Del Rio Bar.
22. Failing to question important witnesses in the burglary at New Mexico A&M College.

(Paraphrased from *LCSN* July 11, 1949)

As a result of the listed charges and a recommendation that Sheriff Apodaca be removed from office temporarily, pending a trial, state comptroller J. D. Hannah served an order on July 1, 1949, ousting Apodaca from the sheriff's position. State policeman Ben Martinez was appointed acting sheriff (the same Ben Martinez who had been sent to Las Cruces to help investigate the Coogler case). Although Happy Apodaca's attorney, Harry Bigbee, challenged the validity of Apodaca's suspension, Judge James McGhee upheld it. A removal trial, however, would be necessary to remove Apodaca more permanently from office.

The newly energized grand jury returned twenty-nine more indictments on July 7, 1949, most of them for liquor-law and gambling violations. Justices of the peace Ramon Duran and T. V. Garcia were indicted—Duran for embezzling office fines and fees, and Garcia for gambling operations and impersonating a federal judge (*LCSN*, September 4, 1949). The following were charged with selling liquor to minors (including Cricket Coogler in most cases, since her access to alcohol prompted the questions): Bridget Seybold, Airport Inn; Arthur Fountain, El Patio Bar; Bon Hall, Penguin Lounge; A. S. and Fred Barncastle, Gateway Gardens; Clark Hurst, Oasis Club; N. V. and Barbara Ulmer, Clover Leaf Club; and from the Del Rio Bar, W. W. Riley and G. D. Kilcrease (*LCSN*, July 8, 1949). The charges against W. W. Riley, G. D. Kilcrease, and Bon Hall were subsequently dropped (*LCC*, January 12, 1950).

Acting sheriff Martinez, Deputy Sheriff Marcelo Hinojosa, and field agent Roy Sandman went to work serving the warrants. Martinez announced that the sheriff's office would be open twenty-four hours a day until further notice.

Among the grand jury indictments was one that drew special attention statewide, especially in the government buildings. It was against the recalcitrant corporation commissioner, Dan Sedillo, for morals charges involving sexual intent with Cricket Coogler. A trial would be placed on his agenda, and it was expected that he would answer some questions after all.

The grand jury's report criticized eight other officials:

- Judge W. T. Scoggin Jr. for failing to uphold gambling laws.
- District attorney T. K. Campbell for refusing to act on the reports of serious criminal offenses.
- State police chief Hubert Beasley for drinking on duty and ignoring gambling laws. (When asked by a reporter to comment about the charges against him, Beasley said he knew nothing about it.)
- Las Cruces police chief Santos Ramirez for failure to ensure proper law enforcement.
- State patrolman Carlos Salas for permitting gambling violations.
- State patrolman I. E. Salazar for drinking on duty.
- Las Cruces policemen Reuben Flores and Vicente Lucero for gross neglect and incompetence, particularly with regard to the night of the disappearance of Cricket Coogler (Paraphrased from *EPHP*, November 19, 1949).

Throughout their work, the Doña Ana County Grand Jury members were wary of threats and intimidation attempts. R. A. Durio said there was no direct intimidation of him, but on the day of the gambling-house raids, some kind of blanket threat to the jury caused him to phone his wife at home. He asked, "Where are the children?" Mary said, "Playing in the yard." "Don't let them out of your sight," he said. Mary noticed a strange car in the neighborhood that day, for several hours. "I went out and took down the license number and then it went away," she said. "It was from Anapra but we could never find out who the car belonged to" (VI).

The house of another grand jury member, Edwin Kull, also appeared to be under daily surveillance from a strange car parked on their road. When his daughter complained that she was being followed, her mother began to personally escort her home from school (AI).

Byron Darden, one of the grand jury's chosen attorneys, was the intended victim of scare tactics as well. An unknown man forced one of Darden's neighbors and her child, a boy the same size and age of Byron Darden's son John, into his car and took them on a frightening ride, threatening the bewildered woman that she had better tell her husband to lay off, intimating that her husband would know what that meant. Byron Darden was sure the chilling experience had been intended for his own wife and son. A retired neighbor of the Dardens subsequently spent many hours sitting outside his home with a gun, watching the Darden home (AI). Darden had a good many friends, evidenced by an inordinate number of requests for him to be a pallbearer at funerals.

Assistant district attorney E. E. Chavez told a judge that he had received several threatening phone calls warning him not to testify (*EPHP*, July 11, 1949). And as already noted, a number of people had left Las Cruces in the spring and summer of 1949.

Besides psychological stress, members of the grand jury were under a great deal of financial stress. Many of them were employed on hourly wages, and the jury met long hours for nine solid months. Members were paid just three dollars a day, and six cents a mile for travel. Working on percentage for the Buddy Grider Garage, jury member R. A. Durio lost a great deal of work time because of jury sessions. Mary Durio said her family got by with a lot of help from a sympathetic grocer and clothing merchant. She said R. A. "would get through with the jury, go to work until two or three in the morning, get a few hours sleep, and get up and go to the jury again" (VI). Other jury members endured similar hardships. (Mary Durio added a note from her own experience during the grand jury's sessions. She said her parents had some rentals in nearby Ruidoso, and once when she went to visit, one of the tenants came over to pay the rent. Mary's mother mentioned that Mary's husband was on the Doña Ana County Grand Jury, and that night the tenant moved out with no notice whatsoever.)

Here are the closing statements of the Doña Ana County Grand Jury's final report:

The deplorable conditions into which law enforcement had fallen in Doña Ana County was apparent immediately at the beginning of our work.

The records of the official investigation [Cricket Coogler matter] . . . were extremely meager and of very little value to us. The officials themselves were able to add little to the records.

It therefore became necessary for us . . . to [expend] a great amount of time and effort to assemble background information and minor details which should and could have been far more easily obtained immediately after the occurrence of these offenses. . . .

Due to the long lapse of time, witnesses generally could not recall with any particular exactness the details which would have been available with more certainty had prompt and thorough investigations been made when these matters first became known.

We sincerely regret that we were unable to determine just who were the responsible parties for these crimes. We trust that investigations will continue until the guilty parties are brought before the bar of justice. We most strongly and sincerely urge the citizens of Doña Ana County to never again permit the existence of conditions so prejudicial to their rights and welfare as prevailed in our county during the first part of the year 1949. (*EPHP*, November 19, 1949)

In a slap at the local newspapers, the Doña Ana County Grand Jury, when their work was over, sent a thank-you letter to the *El Paso Herald-Post*, which the paper of course printed on its front page of November 23, 1949. The jury wrote: "It is a particular inspiration to see the press striving diligently to right the many wrongs forced upon the people by a few unworthy and neglectful officials. . . . We hope [you] will ever follow the course which you have so properly directed in keeping a watchful eye over our public affairs."

At the end of the day, the Doña Ana County Grand Jury did not point the direction to Cricket's murderer, but that was not their charge. They stood up to the power of a corrupt state network and brought tremendous attention to the Coogler case, much to the chagrin of those working to stifle such attention. They did the county a good service, as *Herald-Post* editor Ed Pooley said:

It [the jury] was the greatest and most effective influence for civic decency in New Mexico's history. . . . They indicted five officeholders. Four of those found it expedient to resign.* The fifth [Dan Sedillo]

---

* These four were Sheriff Happy Apodaca, Anapra justice of the peace T. V. Garcia, county commission chair M. E. Garcia, and justice of the peace Ramon Duran. T. V. Garcia had changed his plea to guilty of gambling, embezzlement, and posing as a federal judge. He received a 90- to 149-day sentence with a two- to three-year suspended sentence. The other Garcia, M. E., pleaded guilty to gambling violation. Ramon Duran served a 120-day sentence for embezzlement, with a three- to five-year suspended sentence (*New York Times*, February 26, 1950).

fights with every technicality a battery of lawyers can muster the charge they filed against him. . . .

Because of the labors of this Grand Jury, a great stillness has settled over all New Mexico. The one-armed bandits no longer whirl, the dice do not rattle, the chips do not click. . . . From the southern border, where the loud-mouthed racketeer bragged "the fix is in from here to Santa Fe" to Taos and Gallup and Clovis and Lordsburg, the atmosphere is clearer and the climate is healthier. The politicos at Santa Fe walk circumspectly. . . .

The grand jury was not able to bring to book the brutal murderer of the little 18-year-old girl, Cricket Coogler. Yet it was the instrument whereby Cricket's short life, whatever its nature, was justified. Without her death the grand jury would not have been called, and without the grand jury, the vileness that ran through New Mexico like a river of filth would not have been stopped.

It is too much to hope that Cricket's killer has a conscience that will trouble him. But perhaps there is enough of his brutish brain for him to retain the memory, all the days of his years, of the broken little body he buried in the desert. And may those who failed to speak out, those who lied, and those who hid away with their cowardice, remember, too. (*EPHP*, November 19, 1949)

Time magazine on August 15, 1949, featured an almost full-page story, with pictures of Walt Finley, Cricket Coogler, and Happy Apodaca. "Last week the state was shaking from the effects of the biggest political land mine which had blown up in years," *Time* said. "The jury had already returned 58 indictments against 25 people, had brought the cold sweat of apprehension . . . to the brows of many a high-placed gambler and politico."

The grand jury's frustration in solving questions about Cricket's death fueled their determination to at least clean up Doña Ana County. Governor Mabry made the rather tardy statement that if local authorities were unable to curb gambling, he would turn the job over to the state police. At the time, the state police chief himself was charged with a civil rights crime in connection with a suspect in the Cricket Coogler case.

Some might argue that in retrospect, simple inexperience was a little-recognized factor in the handling of the Coogler case. The grand jurors were new at their job, district attorney T. K. Campbell was new at his, and

Sheriff Apodaca was new at the sheriff's desk, if not to law enforcement in general.

Ollie Coogler wrote this careful note of appreciation to Doña Ana County Grand Jury foreman Hal Cox, whose personal power and influence had been underestimated by some:

> It is always difficult to say the words of gratitude that a person would like to say in appreciation for services . . . made by fellow men. But please accept this note of thanks in all sincerity from myself and my family for all the kindnesses shown to us. [Signed] Mistress Ollie Coogler & family. (DP)

Ollie Coogler owed few such notes.

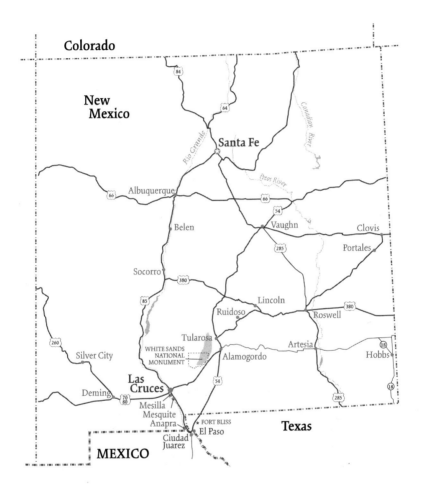

Simplified map of New Mexico, 1949
(University of New Mexico Press).

Aerial photo of Las Cruces, 1950

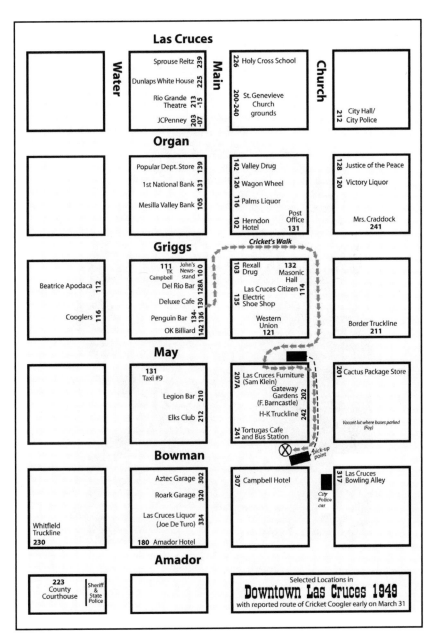

Downtown Las Cruces, 1949

(AUTHOR, THE PRINT SHOP, LAS CRUCES).

Ovida "Cricket" Coogler

Site of DeLuxe Café, 130 S. Main, Las Cruces

(AUTHOR, 2004).

State patrolman Happy Apodaca

Judge William T. Scoggin Jr.

Jerry Smith at approximate location he discovered Cricket Coogler's body
(Author, 2004).

Carpenter's Store, Mesquite, NM

(AUTHOR, 2004).

Doña Ana County Grand Jury member R. A. Durio with son Bobby and wife Mary (AUTHOR, 2004).

Lt. Governor Joseph Montoya as he appeared in the 1947–1948 New Mexico Blue Book
(NM State Records Center and Archives).

Victor Salazar, Dorothy Mechem, woman believed to be the
governor's mother, and Governor Ed Mechem in 1962
(NEW MEXICO STATE RECORDS CENTER AND ARCHIVES).

Chope Benavides (*left*), Marcelo Hinojosa, and two friends
(Courtesy Amelia Rivas).

Roy Sandman and Marcelo Hinojosa

(COURTESY PETER SANDMAN).

8 Politics and Payoffs

The state officials about whom innuendo and suspicion flowed in the Coogler case were Democrats, since in 1949 most of New Mexico's elected officials, and almost all appointed officials, were Democrats. In the thirties and forties, nomination by the Democratic Party pretty much equaled election in New Mexico.

Votes could be bought in New Mexico. Ernest Fincher, in his study *Spanish-Americans as a Political Factor in New Mexico, 1912–1950*, quotes the head of the United Press in Santa Fe as saying that Hispanic votes were bought on a large scale in many counties in the 1948 election, with the price as high as eight dollars a vote. And in 1950 the archbishop of Santa Fe condemned the vote buying and ballot stealing in the state.

Aside from gathering votes, bureaucrats visited Doña Ana County for many other reasons. In the spring of 1949, for example, the New Mexico Cattle Growers Association needed calming. At an Albuquerque meeting on March 29, they announced their opposition to government acquisition of private land for a proposed 3,000-square-mile enlargement of the U.S. Army's White Sands Proving Grounds,* adjacent to the phenomenal White

---

* *Time* magazine, October 31, 1938, had covered a story about a Works Progress Administration (WPA) scandal at White Sands, with charges that Senator Dennis Chavez had placed eighteen relatives on the WPA payroll and collected "contributions" to the Democratic Party from other WPA workers monthly. No convictions resulted for Chavez's family members, although the U.S. Senate threatened to expel Chavez for his part in the scandal.

Sands National Monument. A good deal of the land to be absorbed by the proving grounds belonged to the family of Hal Cox, who would very soon be named foreman of the Doña Ana County Grand Jury.

Senator Dennis Chavez, sometimes called the last of the *patrones*, was the most prestigious and powerful cog in the state party machine. According to political columnist Joe Clark, "Chavez reportedly named more than half of the Democrats who received lush appointments from [Governor] Mabry" (Fincher). Mabry no doubt owed Senator Chavez for some influence in his 1946 election as governor.

In the 1940s, the state's Democratic Party machine had access to aid from at least two state patrolmen: Happy Apodaca and Ernest A. "Tuffy" Tafoya, a chain smoker who usually wore dark sunglasses. Tuffy and Happy, well known simply by those nicknames, had continually traversed most or all state counties as state policemen, knowing well who in each community had the power to deliver votes (AI). The two were regarded by many as tough, powerful, rough, and wild, although Doña Ana County Grand Jury member R. A. Durio and his wife Mary described Tafoya as "a nice guy, one who would help you if he could" (AI). Tafoya's reputation, like Apodaca's, depended on who was doing the talking.

Waitress Katie Etherton remembered a conversation with Tuffy Tafoya about the Coogler case in which she apparently accused him of covering up for Sheriff Apodaca, implying that state patrolmen would always stick up for each other. She said Tafoya took offense and informed her that just because he was related to Happy didn't mean he would cover up anything. "I didn't know he was Happy's cousin," Etherton said (VI).

Governor Thomas Mabry had a gubernatorial look and was generally regarded as classy, showing up in the right places and saying the right things, but he was perceived as wielding little power.

Mabry's lieutenant governor, Joseph M. Montoya, was the son of a sheriff. He was very good looking, with a beautiful smile and compelling dark eyes (impossible to break a mutual gaze, so it was said, until he looked away first). When in Las Cruces, Montoya spent some time in Malone's Drug Store, the unofficial Republican headquarters, extending his influence and keeping abreast of the opposition party's activities (AI). Conjecture had it that he was being groomed for a seat in the U.S. Congress. And indeed he did eventually succeed Dennis Chavez in the U.S. Senate. Montoya shared a distinguished ancestral line with Senator Dennis Chavez, traceable all the way back to the seventeenth century.

Happy Apodaca's brother-in-law, "Hooky" Apodaca, won the race for mayor in the town of Bernalillo in February 1948. Hooky's opponent, James Pitts, was backed by "Little Joe" Montoya and his brother, Tom. It was the brothers-in-law against the brothers, and the Apodacas won.

By the late 1950s, Joseph Montoya, according to Maurilio Vigil's *Chicano Politics*, was to become the most powerful Hispanic politician in the country. But even in 1949, his name already had a high profile and was a target for opponents.

The 1949 state commissioner of the Bureau of Revenue (a gubernatorial appointment) was Victor Salazar, commonly referred to as "the second-floor governor" or simply "the governor," which of course denigrated the powers of Governor Mabry. Victor Salazar's revenue bureau was powerful, acting as final authority on all matters of policy in his twelve divisions, which included Drivers License, Motor Transport, School Tax, Luxury Tax, Severance Tax, Gasoline Tax, Income Tax, Liquor Control, and others. Some said Victor Salazar occasionally issued liquor licenses himself, although his subordinate Tom Montoya (brother to Lt. Governor Joseph) was supposedly charged with that task. Salazar also administered the state's Collection Agency Law, which licensed and regulated the collection agency business. He was treasurer of the state Democratic Party. Powerful money trails passed over Salazar's desk, and he was in a position to dispense favors. With a regal bearing and a supremely self-confident smile, Salazar exuded an impression of power.

Restaurateur Chope Benavides recounted a time when he was the beneficiary of one of Salazar's favors. Benavides remembered Salazar's impeccable dress and air of authority on one occasion when Benavides fell behind on his state sales tax. Benavides phoned corporation commissioner Dan Sedillo, who arranged an appointment with Victor Salazar, after which a grateful Benavides was allowed to pay the debt in installments (VI).

One foundation of Victor Salazar's power was his understanding of the unvarnished realities of state politics, as in this candid explanation of the need to balance the ballot between Anglo and Hispanic candidates. Salazar:

You have to divide your ticket up racially as well as geographically. For example we have an Anglo governor, Spanish-speaking lieutenant governor, Anglo land commissioner, Spanish-speaking corporation commissioner, and Anglo superintendent of schools. We have one Anglo and one Spanish-speaking (U.S.) Senator and one Anglo and one Spanish-speaking Congressman. You have to see who the officials meet and then you have to get a man who won't antagonize these people. For example, since most of the big landowners and oil men are Anglos, the land commissioner must be an Anglo. (Fincher)

If not for "Governor" Salazar, gambling payoffs were collected for someone in Santa Fe, and for law-enforcement officials as well, because so many continued to look the other way when illegal gambling levers were pulled. One witness described the scale of profits on slot machines in several counties this way: "Forty percent went to the owner of the location in which the machine was installed, forty percent to the owner of the machine, and twenty percent to politicians" (Keleher). In 1949, it was estimated that the gambling payoffs totaled as much as $50,000 a year in Doña Ana County (*EPHP*, August 6, 1949).

Another prominent name in state government, state police chief Hubert Beasley, was thrown into the mix when he was dispatched to Las Cruces by Governor Mabry or "Governor" Salazar to look into the Coogler case. While Apodaca was sheriff, the state police used a small space in his office for their Las Cruces headquarters. That brought Chief Beasley into close proximity with Apodaca.

Governor Tom Mabry was due to present an award on Saturday, March 26, 1949, at the Doña Ana County Courthouse. He sent his regrets, however, because his wife and daughter were slightly injured in an automobile accident. Lt. Governor Joseph "Little Joe" Montoya was scheduled instead. It is not known whether Lt. Governor Montoya's stay might have stretched four days into the time critical to the Coogler case, or whether, after the highly publicized protests of cattlemen, a quick return trip for on-site talks about the contentious White Sands land deal might have been proposed.

A few state officials visited Doña Ana County to participate in activities not suited for publicity. If one knew who to ask, the easiest routes to all kinds of gambling and prostitution could be found. If one knew who to ask, any man with an appetite for rough or bizarre sex could find that kind of outlet. (An unidentified background voice taped during the making of *The Silence of Cricket Coogler* claims to agree with political commentator Jack Flynn's view that Joseph Montoya had a reputation for drinking heavily and being rough with women.) Packing for a trip from Santa Fe to Doña Ana County might have resembled a hunting trip: plenty of cash and liquor, but no wives.

If the visitors were looking for girls, reporter Walt Finley could not at first understand what there was about Cricket Coogler that would warrant such attention. He said he felt he knew Cricket as well as anyone, after talking with people about her for months. She was attractive but not a raving beauty, and there must have been girls within a closer radius to Santa Fe who might have sufficed. But Finley said what he learned in later interviews led him to suspect uglier circumstances most girls would not tolerate, involving, for example, bondage. Finley:

Dan Sedillo and Happy Apodaca had tied Cricket to a table in a motel at some time. One other girl had been present. (VI)

About three weeks before her death, Cricket had told friends she had gone to Juarez with another girl, a Las Cruces officer, and a state official (*EPHP*, May 24, 1949).

Another obvious magnet for some visitors to southern New Mexico was the array of gambling houses, whose managers invariably recognized and paid special attention to the politicians, handing some of them payoff money to ensure that their establishments would enjoy protection from raids.

Reporter Alice Gruver acknowledged a well-worn joke that so many judges and lawyers were involved in gambling themselves that at every recess they were off checking on their winnings (VI). Former supreme court justice LaFel Oman, practicing law in Las Cruces at the time, said, "I'm not saying Governor Mabry was involved, and I'm not saying he wasn't, [but gambling payoffs] got right damn close to the governor's office" (*AJ*, February 23, 1986). If "second-floor governor" Victor Salazar actually held the primary power, those who tended first to adopt a follow-the-money theory as the answer to any mystery, including the Coogler case, naturally looked his way. But Victor Salazar remained out of the Coogler case spotlights.

Except for a few token raids, Sheriff Apodaca apparently refused to cooperate with citizens willing to sign affidavits that would justify prosecution of the gambling proprietors (Keleher). Chope Benavides once rode with Apodaca and some state officials (unnamed) to an Anapra gambling house, where he said they were treated royally with fine steaks, etc. He said, "I think we even gave them a case of whiskey as we left" (VI). At the very least, the sheriff was a person the gambling house considered worth courting, and vice versa.

Underworld kingpin Mickey Cohen spent a few weeks visiting some of the gambling houses in the area. Cohen and his burly bodyguard John Stomponato were escorted to the Albuquerque city limits on August 11, 1950. August 30 found them in southern New Mexico. Around two in the morning, an El Paso cab driver took Cohen (traveling under the name of Denny Morrison Jr.) and another man (who also gave his name as Denny Morrison) on a tour of Anapra, since the men had a three-hour wait for a flight to Midland, Texas (*LCSN*, August 30, 1950).

Cohen's stops around Anapra likely included Frank Ardovino's La Loma del Rey*; the Valley Country Club, run by Robert Milkman out of Cleveland; the Sunland Club (renamed Tropics Club), run by Barney Marcus out of Brooklyn; and/or Tom Burchell's place.

Amid lots of gossip and speculation about who paid whom for protection of gambling, FBI informants identified only as T-1, T-2, and T-3 got down to some show-stopping specifics, including the following allegations in the 1948–1949 time period about three Anapra gambling spots:

> Payoffs were being made by the owners of . . . the Valley Country Club, Tom Burchell's, and the Tropics Night Club . . . to . . . Happy Apodaca and Carlos Salas (T-1).
>
> The Tropics Night Club had paid $300 per week . . . to Carlos Salas . . . [and] $1,000 to Happy Apodaca, Sheriff-Elect (T-2).
>
> Sheriff Apodaca admitted receiving at least $300 a month from each gambling establishment at Anapra, New Mexico, and brags that as long as gambling is going to operate in his county, he is going to get his share (T-3). (Paraphrased from NARA3)

---

* In the same location and retaining its vintage appearance, Ardovino's Desert Crossing, a popular restaurant and lounge, is now operated by Frank Ardovino's nephew.

Robert Milkman of the Valley Country Club bore the harshest brunt of the allegations from these confidential informants. It was said that

> [Milkman] paid Lt. Governor Joe Montoya $30,000 to have the Tropics Night Club and Tom Burchell's put out of business, and out of competition, with his club (T-2).
>
> Apodaca also received money from . . . Milkman for his recent campaign for sheriff (T-2).
>
> Milkman paid off . . . Apodaca and other county officials . . . through his close friend and associate Sam Klein, mayor of Las Cruces (T-2).
>
> Milkman . . . paid at least $1,200 a week . . . split three ways: District Judge Scoggin, Sheriff Apodaca, and the remainder forwarded to the state Democratic organization. [Note: At the time, the state Democratic Party chairman was H. R. (Ray) Rodgers, who was also treasurer of the state of New Mexico. State Democratic Party treasurer was Victor Salazar. T-3 cited two Alamogordo men as sources of this information.]
>
> Carlos Salas obtained a cut from instant gambling payoffs, including small locations in the Mesilla Valley. . . . Tommy Campbell was not receiving any payoff money (T-3).
>
> Chief Beasley, . . . Sheriff Apodaca, and other Las Cruces officials [had] been given valuable diamond rings by Milkman (T-3).
>
> A . . . former employee of Robert's Jewelry Store in El Paso (owned by Robert Milkman) . . . observed Hubert Beasley, . . . Carlos Salas, . . . and other members of the New Mexico State Police, . . . as well as William Scoggin, [then] district attorney . . . personally contacting Robert Milkman at the . . . store (T-2). (Paraphrased from NARA3)

Informants T-2 and T-3 also pointed fingers at a few others:

> [T]he owner of Tom Burchell's paid $150 per month to [Las Cruces Mayor] Sam Klein . . . who then in turn gave part of the money to District Attorney William T. Scoggin and Sheriff Santos Ramirez (T-2).
>
> A Ruidoso justice of the peace advised . . . that he had personally

observed William Scoggin, then the district attorney, accepting $2,500 in cash from Ruidoso gamblers for the purpose of allowing them to operate openly (T-2).

Judge Scoggin was in possession of a brand new 1949 Oldsmobile, replacing a 1948 Oldsmobile, which was bought and paid for by gamblers at Ruidoso (T-3).

T-2 said he had "received information from a highly confidential source" that [Hubert] Beasley, prior to becoming a law enforcement officer, had been arrested in Las Vegas, New Mexico, for armed robbery of a gambling game. [T-2 said this source personally saw an official county record of Beasley's arrest.] (Paraphrased from NARA3)

T-1 and T-3 were described by FBI agents as reputable and reliable individuals; T-2 was apparently not well enough known to the agents to allow reliability assessment.

A name conspicuously missing from those alleged payoff recipients was Victor Salazar, unless one automatically includes him in the alleged handling of payoff monies from Robert Milkman to the Democratic organization of the state.

Just because some unidentified people made statements to an FBI investigator does not, of course, make them true. No doubt statements in the FBI files are full of innuendo, gossip, and deliberate misstatements. But greenbacks were certainly being passed to achieve obvious protection. These statements were made by people who were at least in the right place at the right time to personally observe what was happening in 1948–1949. In any case, the informants' statements have lain silent in an FBI file for over fifty years, classified for much of that time, and anyone interested in the Coogler case may now have the privilege of considering them.

Cricket Coogler reportedly visited some of those clubs mentioned in payoff schemes, in the company of some very influential men. She could have felt the power of what she knew and, in an imprudent decision, dared to use that knowledge.

9 Happy Apodaca's Troubles Compound

It was, of course, bad news for Apodaca that the Doña Ana County Grand Jury recommended his removal from the position of county sheriff. Simultaneous troubles surfaced to strengthen that recommendation. On the crowded front pages of newspapers during June 1949, next to a column about the grand jury's investigations, Apodaca was accused of multiple sexual assaults.

On June 8, 1949, a former Las Cruces city judge, Sam Pearson, arrived in Las Cruces, telling reporters about a Canadian woman who was in the United States receiving medical attention for tuberculosis. Shortly after the disappearance of Cricket Coogler, the woman said she accepted a ride to the El Paso Immigration Office with a "Las Cruces officer" because she needed her passport visa extended. She said that on the return trip, she was driven off the road, severely injured, and raped twice (*EPHP*, June 8, 1949; and NARA3). Pearson said he reported the attack to district attorney T. K. Campbell, who took no action. For reasons of his own health, Pearson had declined to take up the case against the officer. Reporter Alice Gruver also talked with the Canadian woman, and both she and Pearson said the woman identified her attacker as Sheriff Apodaca and the obstinate official as T. K. Campbell (VI). The woman also reportedly told the manager of the Herndon Hotel (her temporary address) about the rapes. Again, no action was taken. Pearson said T. K. Campbell told him that he (Campbell) would never prosecute anyone on the testimony of a woman who didn't report such an incident immediately. Pearson said he tried to explain to Campbell that the woman was a visitor from another country, in mortal fear of bodily harm, having been threatened with death if she told about the incident. The woman returned to her home in Canada, but Pearson said he believed she would return and testify if she were guaranteed protection (*LCSN*, June 9, 1949). That did not happen.

Las Cruces Citizen reporter Alice Gruver said that when the story about the Canadian woman's ordeal was reported by the *Santa Fe New Mexican* and the *Las Cruces Citizen*, Apodaca threatened to sue those two newspapers, but he never did (VI).

On June 17, 1949, a seventeen-year-old girl, Alicia C., charged that Happy Apodaca had criminally assaulted her on three separate occasions the previous summer (*EPHP*, June 17, 1949). Alicia C. was employed as a domestic at the home of Joe De Turo, a Las Cruces liquor dealer and friend of Happy Apodaca (*LCB*, April 25, 1990). Alicia said that one Saturday, Apodaca, who had been drinking, came to the De Turos' when she was there alone, entered without knocking, and began to make advances toward her. She said he cornered her in the bedroom, where he pushed her onto a bed just as someone knocked on the door, whereupon Apodaca locked her in the bedroom and got rid of the visitor (later established by Walt Finley as John Alexander, who said he arrived to repair a door, but Apodaca told him to leave and come back some other time). Alicia said Apodaca came back to her, twisted her arms above her head until she gave up, raped her, and left the house. The following week, however, she said Sheriff Apodaca again surprised her inside the house before she knew he was around and raped her twice more. She said she put up such a fight the third time that her dress was badly torn. Apodaca reportedly found the doors locked when he came again to the house a few days thereafter, claiming to have left his hat there, but the young lady said she knew what he wanted. She quit her job, not telling the De Turos of the attacks because she was ashamed, and because of their friendship with Happy Apodaca (DP).

Marjorie White of the Las Cruces Welfare Office called on Alicia and, supposedly because of the impression that the girl could not hold a job, took her to Alamogordo, where she went before an Otero County judge and on October 18, 1948, was committed to the Girls' Welfare Home in Albuquerque. For some reason, Alicia C. was not committed from Doña Ana County, but rather from Alamogordo in neighboring Otero County.

As Alicia C.'s rape story broke, Chief Deputy Sheriff Roy Sandman resigned. He said he quit, effective July 1, to take another law-enforcement job. Under a recent amendment to the New Mexico District Attorney's Act, the legislature had conveniently allowed a full-time field agent for the Third Judicial District to be appointed by district attorney T. K. Campbell. Campbell appointed Roy Sandman for that job. But there was apparently another reason Sandman and Apodaca were separated. Sandman, according to an FBI report, said he was not allowed to conduct the Coogler investigation as he wished (NARA3).

On June 24, 1949, another girl (this one only fifteen years old), Romelia C., came forward via the *Sun-News* to allege that Sheriff Apodaca had attempted to seduce her while she babysat at the De Turos' on June 12, while the De Turos and Sheriff and Mrs. Apodaca were attending a party. She said that at some point in the evening, Happy Apodaca appeared, by himself. She said she ran out the back door and waited until Apodaca left, then went back in the house and locked the door. However, the fifteen-year-old would confirm only that the sheriff "talked bad" to her and offered to bring the girl's sweetheart up from Mexico, in exchange for sex (Darden letter to Attorney Martin Threet, Darden Papers). The girl said Apodaca tried to embrace and kiss her and said he would give her money, but did not otherwise harm her. She told the sheriff she wanted to be a good girl, and that her mother was coming. He left.

In an effort to distance himself from his friend's troubles, Joe De Turo issued a statement to the local paper that he and his wife had explained to the grand jury all they knew about the two girls who were allegedly assaulted by Apodaca in their home, that they were unaware of what the girls claimed to have occurred, but that they were in no way seeking to shield Apodaca.

Apodaca claimed he was being set up. Chief Deputy Sheriff Marcelo Hinojosa told FBI special agent William H. Damon that Lonnie Brown, alias Lee Brannon, had suggested that a trap be set whereby Apodaca could be tricked into a relationship with a woman of a tender age, and immediately thereafter local officers would arrest Apodaca (NARA3). Brown had set up a fictitious painting business, and then left town owing money to several other businesses (*LCC*, July 5, 1949). No evidence about such a trap was reported.

To its already lengthy indictments of Apodaca, the Doña Ana County

Grand Jury added two morals charges: rape, and contributing to the delinquency of a minor. Apodaca's bond of $1,000 was met by Martin H. Herrera and Juan Limon, Las Cruces carpenters; Apodaca's uncle, N. S. Apodaca; and Pablo M. Salcido of Las Cruces, a Texaco service station employee (*EPHP*, July 30, 1949).

These charges underscored Apodaca's reputation as a womanizer, preying on young women, but the two morals charges were tabled. Apodaca's removal as sheriff was the only item to be handled at the first trial. The morals charges were to be scheduled in a second trial, but as it turned out, Apodaca never had to answer to them.

He did, however, answer to reporters, at least in the beginning. Early on, Apodaca had been friendly with reporter Walt Finley, even taking some photos of Walt smoking some special cigars, a gift from Apodaca. As the relentless front-page stories continued, however, Happy cooled the relationship, and in a short time, there was no friendship at all (VI).

Finley pressed on, accepting possible risks that his stories might result in harm to himself. In a videotaped interview, Finley shared some experiences:

> I once received an anonymous call from Las Cruces [from a man] saying he had very important information and would be at the Penguin Bar. I didn't trust the FBI and called Detective Tommy Rascon, a friend, and told Tommy where I was going and if anything happened to me, Tommy should investigate. I was young, ambitious, and took chances I would never have taken later in my career. (VI)

Although in that case no harm resulted, Finley had heard from other journalists what could happen when news stories struck too close to home. Will Harrison, the *Santa Fe New Mexican* editor, told him that a San Miguel County Democrat once backed Harrison up to a wall and nicked his throat with a knife to remind him to be careful writing about corruption in San Miguel County.*

---

* Finley couldn't resist adding a favorite Harrison story about a killing in Socorro, where a deputy shot and killed a town marshal, or vice versa. Will Harrison pestered the sheriff's office again and again about when charges would be filed, etc., until he was finally told, "Oh that's been settled out of court" (VI).

Finley again from videotape:

I was puzzled more than once, as I uncovered certain information, when the informant said he/she had already given that information to Happy Apodaca and Happy had never investigated or followed up. It seemed to indicate that Happy knew who killed Cricket and therefore had a basis on which to decide which information to ignore. No one seemed willing to cross Sheriff Apodaca, except for the Grand Jury.

The night before Sheriff Apodaca was indicted by the grand jury, Finley was staying in Las Cruces's historic Amador Hotel, where he said Happy Apodaca walked into his room and pulled out a pistol. "You so-and-so," Happy said, "I'm going to kill you." Finley said he was frightened because Happy's eyes seemed to confirm the seriousness of that threat, as well as the fact that Happy had been drinking. Finally Finley managed to say, "Well, now, Happy, you can kill me, but if you do, Scripps-Howard will send in a *good* reporter." Those words seemed to register with Apodaca, who in a few seconds holstered the gun and warned Finley to get out of town by the morning. Finley did not go away. He covered the indictments the next day (VI).

Finley eventually concluded, as others had, that the reason Cricket was killed might have been that she had obtained valuable political information about gambling payoffs, and perhaps knew where money was being received in Santa Fe (VI).

Newspapers featured a bit of positive family news about the Apodacas in 1949. The *Las Cruces Sun-News* of April 27, 1949, printed within a small article in its social column: "[the] infant son of Sheriff and Mrs. A. L. Apodaca was christened Sunday. . . . Mr. and Mrs. Joseph De Turo are the god-parents." A celebration barbeque followed at the home of a family member. Only a few days after Cricket Coogler's disappearance, an article mentioned that the sheriff was "driving a handsome new Packard motor car" (*LCC*, April 7, 1949). Another column in August 1949 announced that the sheriff was planning to build a new home (*LCC*, August 9, 1949). Such domestic details were regularly published. For example, divorces, and often the reasons for them, could be found on the front page of the *Sun-News*.

The Cricket Coogler story, and the stories that rippled from it, stayed on front pages so long and in so belabored a fashion that some dreaded to open their newspapers, sick of learning about it, wishing to return to a time when they didn't even know about it. But there the thing lay, month after month, year after year. It is said that Ollie Coogler refused to read any newspaper for a long, long time.

The Removal Trial

Silver City, New Mexico, September 12–17, 1949

What became known as the "removal trial" actually began with the ten charges contained in Apodaca's indictment: (1) gambling; (2) permitting gambling at the Valley Country Club; (3) failure, neglect, and refusal to discharge duties regarding Valley Country Club gambling; (4) adultery; (5) failure to account for monies coming into his hands for keeping federal prisoners at the county jail; (6) while transporting a suspect in the Coogler case to the desert for questioning, leaving the suspect in the automobile and purchasing liquor at the Drive In Bar; (7) failure to keep proper records and receipts; (8) receiving illegal fees (a 30-30 rifle) in exchange for dropping charges against a man named William Lancaster; (9) gross immorality, attempting to seduce a female minor; and (10) gross incompetence or gross negligence in discharging his duties as sheriff. The indictment, titled "Accusations for Removal from Office," was returned in district court before supreme court justice James McGhee (paraphrased from *EPHP*, June 24, 1949). Bond was set at $3,000. Apodaca asked for time to raise the amount after he was arrested, and he raised it, with the help of funds collected on his behalf in Santa Fe. Friend Dan Sedillo announced the fund-raising movement, but said he did not know who was in charge, having received only an indirect telephone message concerning it (*SFNM*, June 27, 1949).

On September 12, 1949, Apodaca's removal trial began in Silver City, about eighty-five miles west of Las Cruces, in the court of Judge C. Roy Anderson because Judge McGhee, like Judge Scoggin, had asked to be excused. Not that many years before, convicts had been hanged just outside the handsome Silver City courthouse, which is still in use today (the courthouse, not the gallows). Old marble is the material of its floors and half its walls. Its sunlit courtroom still has the look of the 1950s, with a traditional jury box and a raised area for the sitting judge.

Happy's brother A. T. and his uncle Nicanor Apodaca were present to offer support; the rest of his family were noticeably, and understandably, absent. Martin Threet and LaFel Oman were attorneys for the state, while the feisty Harry Bigbee served as Apodaca's attorney. Talented and sought after, Harry Bigbee was extremely powerful and therefore described as "cocky as a bantam rooster" (LCC, August 30, 1949). For the trial, Happy Apodaca, upon Bigbee's advice, shaved substantial whiskers he was cultivating for Las Cruces's October centennial celebration and left only a trim mustache. At his smiling and handsome best, Apodaca answered few questions.

Alice Gruver reported that the new Republican governor, Ed Mechem, came into the courtroom near the beginning of the trial, then left to answer a telephone call and never returned.

The Santa Fe New Mexican on July 13, 1949, listed eight counts, not ten, with which Apodaca was charged—the wording of the counts having been refined somewhat, but remaining essentially the same as the grand jury's original list. Attorney Harry Bigbee sought to have the morals charges tried first, but Byron Darden, special grand jury prosecutor, argued that if Apodaca were convicted on those charges, Bigbee could appeal the verdict and hold up the removal trial for a long time (EPHP, August 29, 1949). Bigbee of course denied that he wanted to stall the removal trial, but Darden's arguments prevailed (although Darden did not attend the trial, leaving Martin Threet and LaFel Oman to conduct the prosecution's case).

Bigbee was held in contempt of court by Judge Anderson because he had questioned a Las Cruces constable, W. L. Hill, outside the courtroom about Hill's secret testimony before the Doña Ana County Grand Jury, although the judge had already deemed that information not available to the defense. Bigbee apologized to the court for his inappropriate queries, and his apology was accepted.

Constable Hill's remarkable story illustrated that some gambling-club managers had apparently become so arrogant that they could hijack a constable and take back seized equipment. In December 1948, Constable Hill had seized a trailer-load of gambling equipment at the Valley Country Club and was about to leave when he was arrested by order of Anapra justice of the peace T. V. Garcia. Justice Garcia offered an explanation that some stranger had a complaint against the constable. It was reported that the complainant was Frank Ardovino, saying that the country club was being robbed. Constable Hill was arrested and taken to Garcia's store across the street. While Hill was held there, employees of the Valley Country Club broke the lock on the trailer, removed the machines, and restored them to their previous places. Hill reported the incident to Sheriff Apodaca, but no arrests were made (Statement of an Anapra resident in DP; and *EPHP*, September 14, 1959). The Valley Country Club remained untouched.

Attorney Bigbee protested the selection of the jury on the basis of racial discrimination, producing a photostatic copy of all male voters in Grant County, along with percentage figures for Anglo and Hispanic names. He also had names of the jury panel, with the relative ratio of Anglos and Hispanics selected for jury work. The court held that on the basis of evidence shown, there was no discrimination. Judge Anderson did give Bigbee the right to raise the issue again if he could show any actual discrimination.*

Bigbee then moved to quash all accusations on the grounds that the grand jury of Doña Ana County was improperly selected and that discrimination was evident in the selection of those jurors. Judge Anderson overruled, but noted and allowed Bigbee's objections and exceptions (Archives of the Sixth Judicial District Court).

Testimony finally began. Acting Sheriff Ben Martinez said Apodaca's records on the Coogler case were inadequate, with no detailed reports—just loose telegrams, letters, and lab reports. Deputy Roy Sandman said Apodaca's notes, scribbled on pieces of paper, would mean nothing to anyone except Apodaca.

Among the witnesses called in defense of Apodaca were Robert Scoggin, former Raton policeman, and Mayor Diego Salazar of Española (*EPHP*, September 12, 1949). The names "Scoggin" and "Salazar" stand out, but any family links to Judge Scoggin, Commissioner Victor Salazar, or state patrolman I. E. Salazar were not documented.

Perhaps the most memorable witness was Aurelia McFarland, a former bus ticket agent at the Tortugas Café, with whom Apodaca was accused of adultery. She publicly denied any illegal personal activities with Sheriff Apodaca, but she did recount a party a few weeks before Cricket Coogler disappeared at which she, Happy Apodaca, Dan Sedillo, and Rufus Sedillo (no relation to Dan) drank excessively and spent some time at a motel (*EPHP*, September 15, 1949). She also said that on the very day Cricket disappeared, she had accompanied Apodaca to Albuquerque for

---

* Discrimination, certainly present statewide, could provide a weapon for the defense. For example, in the two largest grocery stores in Santa Fe, one wage scale existed for Hispanic workers, and another for Anglos performing identical labor (Fincher).

the purpose of delivering two girls to a welfare home, and she was home by 1:30 a.m., after midnight had ushered in April 1 (*LCSN*, September 14, 1949). Mrs. Florence Perkins, superintendent of the Girls' Welfare Home in Albuquerque, confirmed Apodaca's arrival there, with two delinquent girls and a woman in the car as well, about 2:00 p.m. on March 31, 1949 (*EPHP*, May 28, 1949).

The Coogler case was not the focus of Apodaca's removal trial. However, Mrs. Perkins's story opened the possibility that Sheriff Apodaca could have been in Las Cruces during the critical early morning hours of March 31 if he and Aurelia McFarland did not leave for Albuquerque until later that same morning, about nine o'clock. The drive to Albuquerque took about four to five hours.

The removal trial was not boring. While the Silver City jury discussed whether to remove him from office, Happy Apodaca, smoking cigars, left the courthouse for a time to shoot some pool in downtown Silver City, his attire highlighted by an Elks Club badge and a pair of green socks.

Apodaca was present, however, for the testimony of Mr. Marion Phillips, who was fined for contempt of court on counts of being under the influence of alcohol and volunteering objectionable information from the witness stand. Phillips stated he had run against Apodaca for sheriff in the last primary election. Bigbee asked who had won. Phillips said Apodaca had won, but by unethical means. His language was apparently disrespectful to the court. Phillips was asked to produce a fine of $50 for his contempt citation, and he asked if the judge would accept a check. The judge asked Happy Apodaca, still technically a sheriff, if Phillips's check was good, and Apodaca vouched for it, even though Phillips had just maligned him on the stand (*EPHP*, September 13, 1949).

Judge Anderson instructed the jury to completely disregard testimony adverse to Apodaca relating to several of the charges: adultery, seduction, failure to account for sheriff's office funds, entering a bar while investigating the Coogler case, failure to take pictures at the scene where Cricket's body was found, failure to make investigation at the time the body was found, or any delays in investigating the Coogler death or the college robbery. All of these charges were dropped for insufficient evidence. The judge also instructed the jury that if they found "that any act or acts that the defendant is accused of were committed after December 31, 1948, you shall find the defendant not guilty even though you should further believe that the defendant committed such act or acts prior to such date" (Archives, Sixth Judicial District Court). That meant that the tale about Cricket's ordeal of being tied to a table in a motel earlier in December 1948, or any other alleged offense committed prior to December 31, 1948, was erased from consideration. The jury was left to consider only whether Apodaca was guilty of gambling, permitting open gambling, taking an illegal fee from a prisoner, and a general charge of gross incompetence and negligence in his official duties (*LCSN*, September 15, 1949).

On the afternoon of September 17, 1949, after twenty hours of deliberation, the jury was dismissed when it failed to yield a verdict. Unanimity was a requirement. The jury deadlocked at a vote of seven to five (*EPHP*, September 17, 1949). The jurors were:

- Tommy Jimenez, Silver City laborer
- Arthur A. Caballero, Mimbres rancher
- Steve Peru, Silver City miner
- Reges J. McSherry, Mimbres rancher
- Marcelle K. Biebelle, San Lorenzo rancher
- Bob L. Hubbard (alternate)
- Joseph B. McDonald, Pinos Altos miner
- Felix Sandoval, Silver City grocery clerk
- Sam Phoenix, Silver City cattle buyer
- Alvin E. Franks, Silver City oil distributor
- Clifford Renick, Chino mine blacksmith
- Homer Stewart, Chino shovel operator
- William Chaney, foreman, Chino mine electrician

Judge Anderson declared a mistrial.

Apodaca went free, but Judge Anderson immediately ordered a retrial in the city of Tucumcari, on the plains of eastern New Mexico, scheduled for October 18, 1949, where Apodaca would face six charges, to be followed by a separate trial on criminal charges of rape. Attorney Harry Bigbee suggested Albuquerque as a preferable location away from the public excitement. He stated that his client would suffer prejudice at the Tucumcari location, suggesting ethnic discrimination on the eastern side of the state, and that even transferring the trial back to Doña Ana County would be a better alternative than Tucumcari (Archives, Sixth Judicial District Court).

On October 6, 1949, Happy Apodaca was back in his office following an order from state comptroller J. D. Hannah reinstating him as sheriff of Doña Ana County. A crowd of back-slapping friends followed him inside to his office in the big white courthouse, some shouting out, "Didn't I tell you?" (*EPT*, October 6, 1949). The euphoria lasted only a few days. On October 11, 1949, as his community began lavish centennial celebrations, Apodaca was once more ex-sheriff, this time as a result of his own resignation.

Attorney Harry Bigbee had denied that his client would resign if the state dismissed all charges, but that is exactly what happened. T. K. Campbell announced that by agreement, all charges against Apodaca, both civil and criminal, were dropped (*EPHP*, October 12, 1949). Editor Homer Gruver of the *Las Cruces Citizen* saw it this way: "I believe . . . reinstatement by Hannah was part of the prearranged plan of the state and defense lawyers" (*LCC*, October 13, 1949).

Bigbee explained Apodaca's resignation to reporters differently:

The resignation idea just arose naturally out of a conversation with Martin Threet at a meeting of the State Bar Association at Tucumcari over the weekend. It's hard to say just who, if anybody, first put forth the plan. (*EPHP*, October 12, 1949)

Las Cruces Citizen editor Homer Gruver wrote on November 8, 1949, that "tremendous political pressure was brought to bear" on both Threet and Bigbee. Therefore, Bigbee had suggested that perhaps it would be wise to seek a compromise in the case, since all subsequent trials would result the same as the Silver City trial—in a hung jury. (After all, Gruver pointed out, it took only one dissenting voice to hang a jury in New Mexico.) Bigbee reportedly also proposed that it would save the county thousands of dollars if the case could be compromised, so he (Bigbee) "was quite willing to end the case because of the sad state of Happy's personal financial condition." "Mr. Threet apparently thought there was some logic in [these] arguments . . . [and] the result was that an agreement was reached; and Mr. Bigbee told Mr. Apodaca to resign" (*LCC*, November 8, 1949).

Apodaca, by resigning his post, avoided a second removal trial, as well as another trial on two criminal charges of rape and contributing to the delinquency of a female minor. Arguments as to location for a retrial became moot. This did not please the citizenry. Regardless of Apodaca's sad financial state, they saw that, indeed, trial for crimes could be escaped simply by resignation from a political position.

State policeman Ben Martinez, who had been acting as interim sheriff, returned to his state-police duties, and Jose Viramontes was appointed sheriff on October 14, 1949. Sighs of relief likely were heard the morning Viramontes took over. He was a respected old-school gentleman who tipped his hat to ladies, and it was said that if Viramontes drove the sheriff's car on unofficial business, even to get a hamburger, he subtracted that mileage from any reimbursement request. He never wore a gun, and he continually held a small, never-lit cigar in his mouth. In a surprise move, Viramontes requested that Roy Sandman be released from his present duties in the district attorney's office and assigned "to assist him in his office" (*LCC*, October 18, 1949).

In the June 1950 primary election, Apodaca challenged Jose Viramontes for the sheriff's position but was defeated soundly, with only one precinct—Anapra 17—going to Apodaca. The little semiweekly *Las Cruces Citizen* offered some barbed opinions about that election:

> The fact that A. L. "Happy" Apodaca had the audacity to become a candidate at all bespeaks a carelessness of public opinion which is unhealthy, to say the least. . . .
>
> The man on the streets of Las Cruces treats "Happy" Apodaca as simply an amusing person. "Oh him? What a character!"
>
> Whether deliberate or accidental, this type of humor is one of the most disarming methods of mass psychology.
>
> Mr. Apodaca, as representative of the cauldron of corruption that is New Mexico politics, is about as funny as a stiff case of polio—and as dangerous. (*LCC*, June 2, 1950)
>
> He [was] asking for a public verdict, something he was afraid to ask of a jury. He [was] asking for the people's vindication or condemnation. . . .
>
> Insofar as the robbery . . . [at A&M] and the subsequent murder of Ovida Coogler, except the fact that they did occur, nothing has been proved other than at the time of their commission we apparently had a set of public officials thoroughly incompetent, or totally indifferent to . . . these crimes and the performance of their sworn

duty, or were just naturally, pitifully ignorant or dumb. That is the truth, so why wince from telling it. (*LCC*, February 1, 1950)

Immediately upon his defeat in the election, Apodaca saw an opportunity in Santa Fe, where the city police chief had been removed under a thirty-day suspension. Apodaca wrote a letter to the Santa Fe mayor, with copies to each city council member, asking to be considered for the job in the event a vacancy might occur in the near future (*LCC*, June 16, 1950). He did not get the job.

The strain must have taken a toll on Happy Apodaca, but he apparently still felt himself above the law. In July 1950, another arrest warrant for Apodaca was issued from a Las Cruces justice of the peace, in response to a complaint filed by a Corporal Willie Cahoon of Fort Bliss, Texas. Cahoon said an auto bearing a red police-type light forced him to the side of the road; a man got out of the car and, without provocation, cursed and struck him. Cahoon noted the license number, which was identified as Apodaca's. He also identified Apodaca from a photo. Apodaca said that on July 5, the day the offense was claimed to have occurred, he was working as a carpenter in El Paso and did not use his car during the day. The only outcome: District Attorney Campbell requested Sheriff Jose Viramontes to remove the red light from Apodaca's car, since Apodaca was no longer sheriff and lacked authority to use such emergency equipment (*EPHP*, July 13, 1950).

10 Jerry Nuzum

In the general election of 1950, Edwin L. Mechem, a Las Cruces lawyer and former FBI agent, was elected the first Republican governor of New Mexico since 1933. Immediately, he fulfilled a campaign promise to reopen the Cricket Coogler case. "It can and will be solved," he said (*SFNM*, November 10, 1950).

Governor Tom Mabry was ineligible to succeed himself, but had announced that Democratic candidate John E. Miles certainly would be his successor in a landslide victory (*LCC*, October 12, 1950). The vote was expected to run along in the same way it had for years, with easy Democratic victories. Instead, the 1950 general-election outcome was a shock.

Mechem enjoyed the powerful but indirect support of U.S. Senator Dennis Chavez after Chavez's brother David was defeated in the primary. Chavez could not openly back a Republican, but he could temper his influence on behalf of Miles with the same result. Early on, Governor Mabry exuded overconfidence in a letter to Senator Chavez: "I am sure you will be here to help us out in the general election, and if you do we will have no trouble at all. . . . Sam Klein could never get right and be happy, so we now have our friends to deal with there, and will do all right" (Dennis Chavez Papers). Senator Chavez chose his words carefully as he replied:

Like you I feel that the Republicans are feeling a little cocky but I do not know whether they would be able to get over their general political stupidity. . . . There is no reason why you should not feel confident of reelection, provided of course, that the trend is not too strong. . . . It is my hope to be in New Mexico when the convention takes place. . . .

Now Tom, it is alright [*sic*] to feel confident but please do not take everything for granted. . . . I tried and believe that I succeeded in straightening out a couple of parties from the Southwestern part of the state. . . . I have a pretty good idea of the Doña Ana County situation. Three personal and political friends of mine were elected to the Commission and for this I am most happy. (Dennis Chavez Papers)

Senator Chavez understood well the problems and corruption in the New Mexico government, and many along its chain regularly consulted him on a myriad of issues. He was probably one of the best-informed people in the nation about the case of Cricket Coogler.

After the election, Senator Chavez named the unsolved Cricket Coogler murder as a contributing influence to the Democrats' defeat. He said he hoped the new governor would clean "barnacles and leeches" out of the statehouse—a stinging criticism of the appointments of Tom Mabry (*SFNM*, November 10, 1950). The irony was that Chavez himself had been accused of directing many of those appointments.

New governor Ed Mechem settled into office in January 1951 and immediately set out to make good on his campaign promise to solve the Coogler case. He focused on one person: Jerry Nuzum.

Jerry Nuzum was born and raised in Clovis, New Mexico. He graduated from Clovis High School in 1941. He spent four years in the navy. Jerry's wife Mary was a beautiful blonde with delicate features, invariably described in the many news stories as "pretty," "very attractive," "comely," etc. Every press photo of Mary proved the point. The Nuzums had two little girls, ages three and one, whom his wife said he adored.

Jerry sometimes made the rounds in Las Cruces with Happy Apodaca's crowd or with football teammates. Nuzum said if football players encountered Apodaca in a restaurant, for example, the sheriff usually made a fuss over them and paid for their dinner and drinks. Nuzum said, "At that time I thought the world of him. You couldn't hardly dislike the guy. . . . I never realized he had another side" (VI).

Nuzum was proud of his new car, a maroon 1949 Mercury sedan. How well he knew Cricket Coogler was not determined, but he was with her in the wee hours of the morning of March 31, 1949, the most critical hours of her life, and he would be tried for her murder. Nuzum was in for two ordeals—his initial arrest in 1949, after which he was released, and his second arrest in 1951, which was followed by a trial for murder.

The 1949 Arrest

In the first week of May 1949, Jerry Nuzum, at his job at Levine's store in Clovis, was approached by a state patrolman stationed in Clovis, James Clark, and informed he was wanted in Las Cruces for questioning about the Cricket Coogler case. Clark said Nuzum appeared "pale and nervous," but agreed to voluntarily return to Las Cruces (*LCSN*, June 28 and 29, 1951).

Jerry Nuzum quickly declared his innocence:

> I didn't kill Miss Coogler. Lots of people are angry about the killing. The sheriff had to arrest someone. I was a friend of his. Looks like he selected me to be the fall guy. . . .
>
> The New Mexico State Police Officers keep asking me why I ran my car over Miss Coogler. I keep telling them I didn't.
>
> The officers tell me they discovered . . . blood on the right front spring and the rear spring of my car when they examined it in Santa Fe. While driving from Las Cruces to Santa Fe to have my car examined, a car driven by Sheriff Apodaca hit a chicken. My car was close behind the sheriff's and ran over the same chicken. If they found any blood on the springs of my car, it was chicken blood. Captain Ben Martinez told [me], "We found blood and skin two inches long and one-half inch wide on your car. Why don't you confess?" Even if I had run over Miss Coogler, the blood wouldn't still be on the car. I washed the car twice and a man at the Barnett Oil Company at Clovis washed it two times before it was examined at Santa Fe. (*EPHP*, May 7, 1949)

Nuzum did not appear worried about any material that might be found under his car, but rather more concerned about when and if charges would be filed against him. He said:

[District Attorney] Campbell advised me not to get a lawyer or he would be forced to file charges against me. . . . He told me it would cost a lot of money to hire a lawyer, besides facing the murder charge. So I'm staying in jail of my own free will. (*EPHP*, May 7, 1949)

Regardless of what Campbell had told Nuzum, days wore on and he was neither released nor charged with anything.

Initially, Nuzum had been kept in the more comfortable jailer's quarters in the Doña Ana County Courthouse, then sometimes in a cell, and finally, as Nuzum quotes made the headlines for several days, he was placed in solitary confinement. One day, reporter Walt Finley simply had walked purposefully past the jailer, who probably thought him an attorney, and spied Jerry behind bars. After a few minutes of conversation, Finley was asked to leave. He found Mary Nuzum in the hallway, and she agreed to take her husband a long list of questions.

Nuzum was told he must go to Santa Fe for questioning, and he requested a truth-serum test. He was told it could be arranged. Since Nuzum was now unavailable to reporters, Mary Nuzum described what happened on that trip to Santa Fe:

They asked us to be at State Police Headquarters [in Santa Fe] at 1 p.m. . . . Officers asked us to stay inside the building while they finished examining Jerry's car.

No one said anything to us until about 4:45 p.m. Then, the officers led Jerry to a small office. About 30 minutes later they asked me to come in. . . . Jerry told me the . . . police said they had found skin and blood. . . .

I know the blood they discovered was probably from a chicken . . .

Jerry had also told me he had hit a cat with his car driving from Clovis to Littlefield earlier in the week. (*EPHP*, May 9, 1949)

The truth serum was never administered to Nuzum. His explanation was that he had requested that a family friend, a doctor in Santa Fe, be present with him when the drug was administered, a witness to protect his interests while he was under the influence of the drug. His request was denied, so Nuzum refused to take the drug (VI).

The disappointed Nuzums were informed that Jerry would be returned to Las Cruces for further questioning. Since his car had been completely dismantled at police headquarters in Santa Fe, Nuzum rode back to Las Cruces, again voluntarily since he still was not formally charged, in the company of state police captain Ben Martinez and officer Nolan Utz. These two officers came from the investigative branch of the state police headquarters in Santa Fe.

Mary Nuzum refused a ride back to Las Cruces with Sheriff Apodaca, since it meant she would be traveling alone with him. She bought a bus ticket and arrived in Las Cruces at 5:30 a.m. on Thursday, May 5, 1949.

Patrolman Nolan Utz made this rather careful statement to the FBI about the car search: "Under orders from my superiors I assisted in the search of the automobile of Nuzum. Thereafter in the office of the chief of the state police Nuzum was advised by the chief, Hubert W. Beasley, as to what had been found" (NARA3). It is interesting that Utz offered nothing about what, if anything, he himself saw on or in the car, nor did he indicate concurrence with the blood and tissue findings Beasley reported to Nuzum.

As patrolman Utz drove Nuzum to Las Cruces, Nuzum commented, "I thought a man was innocent until proven guilty," upon which Utz replied, "Not in this state" (NARA4). This same patrolman, Nolan Utz, after only eight weeks of work on the Coogler case, was transferred from Santa Fe to Tucumcari on "special assignment" (*LCSN*, July 3, 1949).

Questioning of Nuzum continued in Las Cruces, including one marathon session lasting from 10:00 a.m. to 4:00 p.m. Sheriff Apodaca, District Attorney Campbell, and the two Santa Fe officers, Martinez and Utz, also listened to recorded statements taken by state patrolman Carlos Salas, who had interviewed several Las Cruces residents. Apodaca advised Nuzum to plead guilty to manslaughter, and Campbell reiterated that if Nuzum did not do so, he would be charged with first-degree murder.

Besides the stories that Nuzum tried twice to get Cricket Coogler into his car on Main Street early on the morning she disappeared, Lamar Bailey, a friend of Nuzum's consistently identified as a "former convict," told a story that seemed to implicate Nuzum. Bailey told state police captain Al Hathaway that he was asleep in the back seat of Nuzum's car "about the time" Cricket disappeared. When he awoke, he said, he found Nuzum driving and Cricket sitting next to him. Bailey was unable to remember the exact date, but investigations appeared to rule out March 30–31, 1949 (*EPHP*, April 7, 1951). Jerry's brother, Bill Nuzum Jr., a jewelry salesman from Albuquerque, attempted to clear up Bailey's statement this way:

Jerry and Bailey had gone to El Paso on Sunday [March 27] and drank. I arrived at Jerry's apartment around noon on Monday [March 28] . . .

I found Bailey asleep on the couch in the front room. Mary, Jerry's wife, will also remember this too. She was angry about Bailey being asleep on the couch.

Jerry said Bailey wanted him to run the swimming pool at Radium Springs. Bailey was manager of a hotel at Radium Springs at that time.

I told Jerry I didn't think he should work for Bailey. He agreed.

Seems like Jerry was having a rough time financially and couldn't keep up the payments on his new car.

I had a friend in Albuquerque where Jerry could get started in the insurance business and still play professional football in the winter.

I went to El Paso on Monday. My wife flew down to meet me Monday night. We stayed at the Hilton Hotel Monday and Tuesday. We came back to Las Cruces about 10 a.m. Wednesday [March 30], the night Cricket disappeared.

Jerry had decided to take the insurance job and they had already packed dishes and everything. (*EPHP*, April 7, 1951)

Bill also offered an explanation about why the Nuzums, although packed and ready to leave, did not leave Las Cruces on Wednesday, March 30:

The only reason Jerry stayed Wednesday was to await an insurance adjuster's check. Jerry's car had been struck by another car while parked in front of his apartment.

They waited until the next day [Thursday, March 31]. They arrived in Albuquerque about 5:30 p.m. Thursday as planned.

The next day, Friday, we went out to a fellow's office. Jerry filled out the application form and they gave him some instruction books. After reading the books Jerry decided the insurance job wasn't his field.

Three days later Jerry and his family drove to Clovis to visit Mother and Dad. While there he was offered a job as a clerk at Levine's.

Jerry called and said one of his friends would be unhappy if he accepted the Clovis job. I told him I didn't think he would be.

Frankly, my main idea was to get him away from Lamar Bailey.

About a week later a fellow offered Jerry a job as a nursery sales-man at Littlefield, Texas. He accepted. (*EPHP*, April 7, 1951)

The story that Jerry Nuzum's car was hit in front of the Nuzum apartment during these critical days apparently prompted little curiosity. Neither the date of this accident nor the identity of the driver were given. If repairs were performed, evidence might have been lost.

As expected of a brother, Bill insisted on Jerry's innocence:

Jerry wasn't running from anything. He had planned to leave Las Cruces before Miss Coogler ever disappeared. I was with Jerry the next four or five days after the girl disappeared. I know if Jerry had anything to do with it I would have known it. I know him like I know my hand. . . .

Jerry had a lot of friends in Las Cruces. He was out saying good-bye to them. That's why he wasn't home with his wife and children. (*EPHP*, April 7, 1951)

Cricket Coogler was in El Paso the evening of March 27, and apparently Nuzum and Bailey were too. Any evening trip to El Paso with Lamar Bailey may well have been for an innocent reason, but it is easier to speculate that it was not for anything wholesome. Could Nuzum and Bailey have been at the Green Frog Café? Could Nuzum have been the "husky soldier," described by Josie Talamantes and Corinne Massingale, who never could be found and whose nickname was written on the back of a photo ticket?

Bailey was certainly less than a reliable witness, but so many of Nuzum's statements, particularly that he did not know Cricket until the night of March 30, 1949, would be invalid if Bailey was telling the truth about wak-ing up in a car with the two of them.

Jerry's brother Bill says the Nuzums were all packed up to move on March 31, 1949, the very day Cricket Coogler disappeared, and Nuzum withdrew from New Mexico A&M that day (*LCSN*, April 9, 1951). The timing of this withdrawal certainly appears suspect. Nuzum gave as a reason the high cost of his classes. But why leave March 31 when the semester in which he had already invested so much effort, with expenses subsidized by the GI Bill, would end in May, only a few weeks away?

Throughout the odd trip to Albuquerque with his brother, Nuzum could be described as somewhat distracted—consenting to an interview, then unable to concentrate on insurance materials, refusing the position, and then delaying three days before taking his family to Clovis, on New Mexico's eastern border, where his parents lived. Nuzum needed a job. Whether anyone confirmed Nuzum's interview with an Albuquerque insurance agency was not revealed.

In Clovis, a more logical destination for him, Nuzum took the temporary job at Levine's Department Store.

On May 10, 1949, District Attorney Campbell made this surprise announcement, amazing in its assumptions, that freed Nuzum:

> Jerry Nuzum has been released from custody this date 1 p.m. A thorough investigation having been made and the statement of Jerry Nuzum checked in detail, it is felt by this office that there is insufficient evidence to longer hold Jerry Nuzum in connection with the death or murder of Ovida Coogler. The statement of Jerry Nuzum after checking in detail was found to be true. . . . It has now become official that the substance found under Nuzum's car was not human flesh. . . .
>
> Jerry Nuzum has definitely been cleared of in any way being at fault or having any guilty knowledge of the death of Ovida Coogler, and insofar as this office is concerned is completely exonerated. (*EPHP*, May 10, 1949)

To Jerry Nuzum, who reportedly had lost twenty pounds pacing in his cell, it sounded official. It came from the district attorney. Jerry thought his nightmare was over, and he and his family celebrated. He found a new job in Littlefield, Texas (not far from Clovis, New Mexico) at Southwest Nurseries and prepared to return to practice with the Pittsburgh Steelers. He thought the matter had ended.

The 1951 Trial

Two years later, on Thursday, April 5, 1951, Nuzum had been scheduled to give a speech at Western Pennsylvania State Penitentiary on "Athletics and Morality," when he was approached and arrested by state police captain Albert H. Hathaway and patrolman Tuffy Tafoya. Nuzum waived extradition and again returned voluntarily to Las Cruces to face a charge that he had killed Cricket Coogler two years before. The two policemen allowed Nuzum to pick up some clothes at his home; speak to his shocked parents, who happened to be visiting; and say good-bye to a crying Mary.

The trip took three days, with the three men sharing hotel rooms. Apparently the policemen had no fear of Jerry Nuzum, leaving their guns on the motel beds as they showered, etc. Nuzum said Hathaway played the good cop, attempting to ingratiate himself by badmouthing Sheriff Apodaca, while Tafoya played the bad cop, threatening tough treatment such as making Nuzum ride to Las Cruces with his arms handcuffed under his legs. On the second night of the trip (a Friday), Nuzum said the two cops placed him in the Jefferson City, Missouri, jail so that they could attend a party (VI). The exhausted officers and Nuzum did not arrive in Las Cruces until Sunday, April 8, about 9:30 p.m. Captain Hathaway explained, "We'd have been here sooner but the police special Ford we were traveling in burned out a generator in the Hondo Valley and delayed us" (*LCSN*, April 9, 1951). Understandably, the alleged party in Missouri was not mentioned.

When Nuzum's second arrest was made public, Apodaca, no longer sheriff since his resignation, said, "I think the state officers have the right man. I questioned Nuzum extensively. I was convinced of his guilt at that time but was unable to shake his alibi" (*LCSN*, April 8, 1951). If Apodaca really was convinced of Nuzum's guilt, why then should it have been necessary to try to coerce a confession from other men, as he reportedly attempted in the spring of 1949?

Nuzum pleaded not guilty at his arraignment on April 9, 1951. A June 26 trial was set, but not without complications.

The state assistant attorney, Walter Kegal, a surprisingly prestigious aide, was sent down, perhaps by the governor, to help fledgling district attorney T. K. Campbell with the prosecution. Kegal began by filing a motion to disqualify Judge Dan T. Price from conducting the preliminary hearing, citing that Price was prejudiced in the case. It was true that Price had said publicly, "The police still haven't got the guilty person, but Nuzum's arrest may lead to the right one. . . . In my opinion, a high state official and a former Las Cruces law officer were involved" (*EPHP*, April 21, 1951). Price was out. The hearing took place in the spectator-packed courtroom of Judge W. T. Scoggin Jr., who apparently was deemed free of such prejudices or leanings about the Coogler case.

Judge Scoggin disqualified himself after the hearing. At Judge Scoggin's request, Socorro judge Charles Fowler of the Seventh Judicial District took the bench as Nuzum's trial began. Hopes for closure in the case had Doña Ana County on its toes, listening, reading.

Charles Margiotti, former attorney general of Pennsylvania and a prestigious lawyer with a record of twenty-six consecutive acquittals for persons charged with murder, initially agreed to defend Nuzum. However, Margiotti's fee was $10,000 plus expenses. Nuzum said he decided he could not afford that high-powered an attorney (VI). Refusing to discuss the reason, Margiotti withdrew from the case June 14, 1951, and locals W. A. Sutherland of Las Cruces and Charles Owen of El Paso were entered as Nuzum's defense attorneys. Interestingly, Senator Dennis Chavez was well enough acquainted with Charles Margiotti that five years earlier he had sent a vague note, saying that if Margiotti came to Washington, to please call him because he needed to talk to him (Dennis Chavez Papers).

Jerry Nuzum's trial began on June 26, 1951, at the Doña Ana County Courthouse, in a heat wave in which temperatures soared to as much as 108 degrees in Las Cruces. Nuzum expressed appreciation that his brother Bill had dedicated his own life and his own bankbook to help pay the attorneys. Bon Hall, proprietor of the Penguin Bar, contributed to Nuzum's cause as well. Cookie Bamert of Muleshoe, Texas—sister of Cricket—sat in the front row throughout the trial. Ollie Coogler had attended only the May 11 preliminary hearing, shielding her face from photographers with a small purse. Former sheriff Happy Apodaca had also avoided photographers by entering through a side door to listen to the preliminary-hearing testimony.

The first witness in Nuzum's trial was Luther "Mr. Green Eyes" Mosley. He and other witnesses who had testified in front of the Doña Ana County Grand Jury were recalled to retell their stories. And the conjectures began all over again.

On May 8, 1949, the Nuzums' landlady, Eloise Ellis, had phoned the newsroom of the *El Paso Times* to say she had been threatened by Sheriff Apodaca on the previous evening, Saturday, May 7, around 11:30 p.m., as she left the Amador Hotel with friends. Sheriff Apodaca and several city and county policemen were standing in front of the hotel entrance. She asked the sheriff about what was going on regarding Nuzum. He said, "I'm not saying." He asked where she was going, and she answered, "To the Frontier Club to have a drink." According to Ellis, the sheriff then said, "You'd better be careful. We don't want to bring back another dead woman. This is a friendly warning" (*EPHP*, May 8, 1949). Ellis said she considered his words a threat to her life, and drove around the block musing on what he had said. Then she bravely returned, parked her car, approached Apodaca, and asked him what he meant by his statement. He answered, "Oh, just be careful." She said they shook hands and she drove away again (*EPHP*, May 8, 1949). Apodaca denied that his conversation with the woman could be interpreted as a threat.

Eloise Ellis was again frightened temporarily as she accompanied Mary to visit Jerry Nuzum at the jail. Sheriff Apodaca locked her and Mary in a cell for several minutes, without apology or explanation.

Eloise Ellis was married and renamed Eloise Brown by the time of the 1951 trial. She repeated her description of Nuzum's honking his car horn, at which time she looked out a bathroom window and saw Mary trying to get Nuzum in the house. Her initial statement in 1949 had been that she looked at the time and it was 2:55 a.m. After close questioning by state policeman Tuffy Tafoya, Eloise Brown acknowledged that she could have been mistaken about the time. State police chief Joe Roach (who had succeeded Beasley by the time of the 1951 trial) declined "to tell the basis for the change or to reveal the time of Nuzum's arrival now fixed by Mrs. Brown" (*EPHP*, April 6, 1951). At any rate, the landlady had withdrawn her support of Jerry Nuzum.

Jerry said that when he arrived home, he knew he was in trouble with his wife, so he decided to "take the offensive and act like I was mad at Mary. I honked the horn and sat in the car and honked again. Then she came out and I put my arm around her. She was not in the best mood in the world" (*EPT*, June 29, 1951).

Mary confirmed his account:

Jerry parked his car beneath our landlady's window about 2:40 a.m. When Jerry gets to drinking he likes to make me mad. He honked his car horn twice. . . . I went outside and it took me about ten minutes to get him inside the house and in the bed. First, he wanted something to eat, then he didn't. The only thing he said to me was, "Honey, don't believe that man." I guess he was talking about the night café manager. (*EPHP*, May 7, 1949, and April 6, 1951)

Mary said also, "I asked him where he had been; he said he had been out with friends. . . . We didn't have an argument. It appeared he was intoxicated" (*EPHP*, June 29, 1951).

A Las Cruces telephone operator, Mrs. Charles Amis, surfaced for the trial. She said she saw one of the altercations in front of the DeLuxe Café, heard Nuzum talking on the telephone, and asked her companion about the time. Her companion answered that it was 3:05 (*LCSN*, June 27, 1951).

State patrolmen Hathaway and Tafoya told a reporter that they had obtained evidence that Cricket was pushed from, or run over by, a speeding car. No details of this evidence ever appeared. The officers at that time theorized that Cricket jumped from a lead car in which she and a well-known New Mexico figure were riding, and was struck by Nuzum's 1949 Mercury convertible (*EPHP*, April 6, 1951).

Any blood or skin purportedly found under Nuzum's car was of course vital to the case. Criminologist Dr. Dwight Rife contended that the matter found under Nuzum's car was human flesh, not animal flesh (*EPHP*, June 27, 1951). Two blood samples were sent to the Texas Department of Public Safety by district attorney T. K. Campbell. The first was negative, cited in a May 10, 1949, letter addressed to police chief Beasley, contradicting Dr. Rife's finding:

[T]he tissue and blood . . . does not respond favorably to tests for human protein. Also no hair of human origin was detected in the sample. (*EPHP*, June 27, 1951)

In a second letter (dated June 11, 1951), requested by Governor Mechem, the agency hedged slightly:

The specimen received in this office . . . was limited in quantity and contained considerable amounts of grease and other material . . . which presented interference in the test. . . . It is not possible to state that the specimen . . . did or did not contain human protein. (*EPHP*, June 27, 1951)

It was unusual for a governor to personally request a second test from the same lab, but this governor, himself a resident of Las Cruces, was attempting to fulfill his campaign promise to solve the case. A second analysis, one absolutely positive, would have strengthened the case against Nuzum and thus helped Mechem fulfill his promise. If that's what Mechem wanted, he didn't get it.

Long testimony was heard from Dr. Dwight Rife. Although Rife held no state credentials as a criminologist, Judge Fowler allowed him to remain in the courtroom as an expert witness, because Rife had twenty years of practice as a physician and surgeon and for seventeen years had a crime laboratory in his office. Dr. Rife acknowledged under cross-examination that he had no formal training in criminology, but had studied the subject at home by necessity. The state apparently had no other available criminal expert, so although Dr. Rife was mildly challenged, both sides did accept his testimony as expert (*EPHP*, May 12, 1951).

Dr. Rife first testified that he helped state policemen examine Nuzum's car on May 4, 1949, at state police headquarters in Santa Fe, but on cross-examination said he had not been present when substances were found. Rather, he said, the substances had been delivered to him by state police captain Clinton White. Rife said one of the substances was red grease (DP). When asked if the particles were of the same nature as lipstick, Nuzum's attorney objected, and the attorney rephrased the question, upon which Rife said the substance was similar to red Crayola and there was not enough to determine whether or not it was lipstick (*EPHP*, May 12, 1951).

Photographs, purported to show places on the car where the substance and stains were found, were introduced by the state over the intense objections of Nuzum's attorney Sutherland, who protested that some photos were not of Nuzum's car, and others had not been taken at the time of the investigation by state police. Those objections were overruled by Judge Charles Fowler.

Captain White testified that there was also a five- or six-inch circle indentation on the underside of the fender skirt on the right rear wheel. He said he had to crawl under the car to see it. Under questioning, Captain White said anything could have caused that indentation and he found no traces of hair or other substance on or around it. Captain White described two brownish spots on the passenger-side front door, under the metal strip, but not enough of the substance to test, he said. "While this car was being examined in the shop . . . I recall Nuzum was free and did move about. . . . The only restriction . . . was that we would not permit him to go under his automobile" (NARA3).

Nuzum maintained that if any blood was found, it had to be chicken blood from the trip to Santa Fe. But his wife remembered a cat he had run over. Then Nuzum recalled one other unlikely possibility. He said his car had struck a little black boy in Littlefield, but fortunately had not really hurt the boy. An officer from Clovis produced a written statement from the two-year-old boy's mother, Ruby Mae Land, confirming that the little boy suffered no injuries serious enough to cause bleeding or broken skin. Mrs. Land said that Nuzum kindly took her son to a hospital and gave him a dollar for ice cream (*EPHP* and *LCSN*, June 28, 1951). Nuzum's car had hit an unlikely number of living things in a very short period of time.

It is gruesome to consider, but some of Cricket's blood and tissue could have been planted on the underside of Nuzum's car. As soon as his car went up on the grease rack for examination of the underside, Nuzum was barred from the location. Officer White and another state policeman, Nolan Utz, performed the examination of the car. If Nuzum's car did exhibit any evidence, it remained shaky.

"It was an odd trial," said Nuzum. "The Grand Jury wouldn't indict me. The DA wouldn't prosecute me. And no real evidence was presented against me" (VI).

However, the trial did offer blockbuster testimony from an entirely new surprise witness for the defense, a woman named Mary Foy from El Paso (former resident of Organ, New Mexico, a small town between Las Cruces and White Sands). Foy said she had known Cricket Coogler for some time and had worked with Cricket briefly in the DeLuxe Café (*EPT*, June 29, 1951). She shocked the courtroom by reporting that she and about fifteen White Sands soldiers saw Cricket beaten by two policemen around 3:00 a.m. on the morning of March 31, 1949. Foy said she was in town on March 30–31 and saw Cricket inside the DeLuxe Café before she (Foy) boarded a bus bound for White Sands Proving Grounds. She said the bus, not scheduled to depart until 6:10 a.m., was parked about half a block from Gateway Gardens. Such a bus might have been parked in a vacant lot across Church Street from the HK Trucking lot on the northeast corner of the Church and Bowman intersection, a space often used for bus parking. Here is Mary Foy's story:

I saw Cricket from the bus window walking from the direction of the Post Office. I saw her face. Then I saw two patrolmen in a state police car. . . . [with] a gold seal on the side.

They drove into the vacant lot and parked back of the bus. An officer in a black uniform got out first. Another dressed in khaki was driving. They got out to pick Cricket up. Cricket ran away from them but they caught her. The man in black caught up with her and she kept kicking and fighting. The man in khaki held her.

The one in black pulled something from his pocket and hit her three different times. She fell to the ground. They picked her up and took her to the car. They went off towards the Post Office.

I couldn't tell whether the man used a gun or a blackjack or what. Cricket was hit once on the forehead, once on the side of the head, and then she fell to the ground.

One of the officers—the one in the black—was a heavyset man; the other was a slender fellow. . . . Soldiers in the bus tried to get out to stop the officers. . . . The sergeant bus driver closed the door and wouldn't let them out. . . . "That's a civilian matter; leave them alone," the bus driver said.

Cricket was crying something in what I thought was Spanish. I thought she was saying something like "Let me go." (*LCSN*, June 29, 1951)

Gold shields were the insignia of the New Mexico State Police. Luther Mosley reappeared, now saying he thought the car that picked up Cricket was black, instead of the gray or brown color he reported in 1949, but he did not mention any insignia on the doors. It should be noted that city police were driving a black Chevrolet that night as well. If Foy saw a state police car, it likely was driven by Carlos Salas, a Bataan Death March survivor, or I. E. "Sally" Salazar, the only state policemen stationed in Las Cruces the night Cricket Coogler disappeared. Any state policeman, however, could have been traveling through.

According to Foy, Cricket Coogler was thrown into a police car at nearly the same location the two city policemen reported her voluntary entry into a cream-colored car.

In a dramatic anticlimax, Sally Salazar and Carlos Salas were brought into the courtroom for Mary Foy to identify, whereupon Foy said definitely that Salazar was not one of the men and she did not think Carlos Salas was the other one. Officers Salazar and Salas were questioned about whether they could have been the officers who struck Cricket. Salas said his log book showed he was home in bed by eleven that night. Salazar said the grand jury took his log book, so he did not know where he was that night (*EPHP*, June 29, 1951). If anybody asked whether Al Hathaway or Tuffy Tafoya, Roy Sandman, Happy Apodaca, Nolan Utz, Hubert Beasley, or any other officer fit Foy's descriptions, it was not reported.

Mary Foy said that when she read about the finding of Cricket's body, she went to the sheriff's office at Las Cruces to report the incident, where a large man with a mustache came out of the back office wearing a cowboy hat, white shirt, and dark trousers. Shown a picture of Apodaca, she said that might be the man who told her she would just get herself into trouble if she didn't keep her mouth shut. He also said she'd better get out of town, and she left. She said she had remained silent for two years out of fear.

This story created an energetic but short-lived frenzy. Foy's testimony conflicted with those of others who were downtown that night—McBride, Mosley, Flores, and Lucero. Not one of the dozen soldiers Foy described came forward to back up her story. A Taxi Number Nine driver made a trip to White Sands that night, which might have been unnecessary if bus service truly had been available. Also, Cricket's mother testified that her daughter could not speak Spanish. However, almost everyone in Las Cruces knew at least a few phrases in Spanish. Three White Sands Proving Grounds personnel testified that no one was allowed in military buses parked in a Church Street vacant lot in Las Cruces overnight. If fifteen soldiers crowded to the bus windows along with Foy to watch policemen beat up a petite young woman, at least one of them might be expected to come forward to confirm that. Sometime later, however, an unsubstantiated story attributed to an unnamed White Sands Proving Grounds security officer appeared to generally support Foy's version. In it, two policemen told the security officer that they had spotted a very drunk Cricket Coogler downtown on the evening in question and attempted to arrest her. She physically resisted, and in the struggle fell, hitting her head against the patrol car door. They loaded her into the back seat and drove the few blocks to the courthouse. Happy Apodaca's car was parked there. The policemen inexplicably transferred the unconscious Cricket into Apodaca's back seat, apparently figuring all would be well when she woke up. Apodaca at some point entered his car and drove all the way home before noticing that Cricket lay in the back seat. When he found that she was dead, he immediately drove to the desert near Mesquite and dumped the body.

Further muddying the situation, Jerry Nuzum was questioned about a March 23, 1949, robbery at New Mexico A&M. It had been a neat job. Near the dial of a big safe in the business office, a small hole had been drilled and filled with lead. All the robbers did was drill the lead out of the hole, trip the tumblers, and walk away with about $12,000. It was the first time any large amount of money had been placed in the safe. No connection was ever established between Nuzum and the robbery. However, the story remained that the thieves gained entrance because of an opening just large enough to allow passage of a small person. Sheriff Apodaca was cited by the Doña Ana County Grand Jury for failure to question important witnesses in this burglary, namely, the college comptroller and cashiers, as well as the janitors who discovered the loss. William Love, an ex-con, A&M college student, and university-housing watchman for a brief time, was suspected, but no evidence surfaced to link him to the burglary.

State police captain Al Hathaway said he felt the college burglary was an inside job, and that a former bank teller had fingered two other men as the robbers. One former bank teller was Wayne Clawson, who became a "person of interest" in the Coogler case because he was charged with attempted rape in another case. But, in a familiar pattern, questions about the burglary connection led absolutely nowhere, and the identity of the burglar was never determined. The college funds were insured, and claims adjusters brought questions of their own. (In a side note, Ralph Apodaca, the New Mexico superintendent of insurance at the time, was Sheriff Apodaca's brother-in-law.)

After he conducted some interviews concerning the A&M burglary, an insurance adjuster reported to his company that (1) Cricket Coogler had arrived home in a beaten condition about two weeks before her disappearance, (2) Cricket told her mother she had been threatened for some knowledge she may have had about the A&M burglary, and (3) Cricket had been talking about this burglary the night she disappeared (Darden Papers). The questioning of Nuzum about that burglary explored another possible link between him and Cricket Coogler, but investigators uncovered nothing to solidify that.

A repeated frustration for investigators, attorneys, and journalists throughout cases linked to Cricket Coogler was that when anyone referred to "the night of March 30," the date was used fuzzily, often without cognizance that at midnight, in a seamless progression of time, the calendar date changed to March 31.

Nuzum's trial was brief—four days, ending on June 30, 1951, when Judge Charles Fowler of Socorro announced that he found it obvious that no case had been developed and therefore directed the jury to find Nuzum not guilty. Judge Fowler told the jury his decision was based on the lack of any evidence of any connection between Nuzum and Cricket's death, and added that it would be an insult to their intelligence to ask them to speculate or guess (*AJ*, June 30, 1951). The jurors were:

- Tomas C. Avalos, farmer
- Eliseo F. Flores, farmer from Hatch, NM
- John Salopek, farmer
- R. F. Turner, Berino farmer
- Cecil D. Herrell, college employee (radio)
- William B. Seehorn, construction
- Henry O. Gutierrez, construction worker
- Harvey L. Barth, accountant
- George Halla, electrician
- J. C. Brookerson, farmer from Hill, NM
- George Berthelon, State Employment Service, Mesilla Park, NM
- Ira E. Simason, insurance adjuster from Fairacres, NM

Governor Mechem announced in the press that inquiries about the Coogler case would continue, but there would no longer be a supercharged investigation. The governor rationalized that staffing a new police school necessarily cut down on the number of men available for the investigation. He also said that officers would no longer be specially assigned to investigate the case. Mechem made no mention of what was an important part of his statement a year earlier—that the full story of the Coogler killing would be uncovered, and that many actions by high officials appeared to lend credence to a whitewash charge. Another promise to avoid whitewash was abandoned. Governor Mechem turned to other state business.

When asked about follow-up to Mary Foy's surprising story, state police chief Joe Roach sounded indifferent. He told reporters that he had not instructed state police to talk with Foy. "I suppose Officer Hathaway got in touch with her," he said. "He was down in Las Cruces yesterday. . . . It seems to me as though Foy's story was pretty well broken yesterday at the trial" (*EPHP*, June 30, 1951).

When asked if any further investigation about the case from the district attorney's office would be made, T. K. Campbell bristled. "If that question means am I going to question every state policeman in New Mexico, the answer is no" (*EPHP*, June 30, 1951).

From the beginning, reporter Walt Finley had sounded increasingly convinced of the innocence of Jerry Nuzum, and his words had swayed others. Finley himself appeared so knowledgeable and so likeable that it was difficult not to accept his point of view, even though in a case as murky as this one, subjectivity was difficult to avoid. Walt Finley's tenacity, courage, and thoroughness in reporting were outstanding. Unfortunately, the bottom line about what happened to Cricket Coogler remained beyond even Finley's skillful reach.

One other person important to the case, Deputy Roy Sandman, seemed certain of Nuzum's innocence, bolstering Nuzum's spirits with the pronouncement that he "knew flat out" that Nuzum was not the culprit (VI).

Nuzum was acquitted—free again, this time for good. The courtroom erupted into celebration, and the case against him was abruptly over. Nuzum was due to report within a week for training for his fourth season with the Pittsburgh Steelers.

11 Dan Sedillo

Born in Morenci, Arizona, corporation commissioner* Dan Sedillo had lived in Las Cruces prior to his Santa Fe appointment and married a local girl, Emelia Barncastle Finch. Good friend Chope Benavides said Sedillo, who sometimes had difficulty breathing because of lung damage in World War II, often would help people who had been forced to sell their farms or livestock by arranging assistance from the state of New Mexico.

Dan Sedillo, handsome and well known in Doña Ana County, reportedly won his post in the 1951 election by way of a "stooge" candidate—that is, one paid to enter a race with no expectation of winning, but for the purpose of dividing the votes of another candidate, often on an ethnic basis. Victor Salazar, head of the state's Bureau of Revenue, explained it like this:

> In the open primary, we can pull anything. Last year (1948) I told Dan Sedillo that he would win for four-year corporation commissioner, even though Paul Martinez would get a lot of votes and the

---

* One corporation commissioner serving with Dan Sedillo was Eugene Allison, who died in an automobile accident December 7, 1951, before the end of his term. Sixty thousand dollars in cash was reportedly found in a shoebox among Allison's possessions after this death (videotape narrator John Ehrlichman). The other commissioner was Ingram "Seven-Foot" Pickett.

Anglos would pull out the east side. So I gave Lester Davis $500 and told him to campaign in Eddy County (that's an Anglo county). He did and carried the county with 1,200 votes. He also carried Lea, Roosevelt, and the other east side counties . . . , splitting the Anglo vote and allowing Dan Sedillo to carry native counties and get the organization vote in other counties. If Davis's vote had gone over to any of the other Anglo candidates, the Anglos would have won. (Fincher)

Although Sedillo was never named as a suspect in the death of Cricket Coogler, he was the highest ranking state official to be questioned about the case and indicted by the Doña Ana County Grand Jury for lesser offenses having to do with Cricket Coogler. Jury member Russell Soper remembered Sedillo's odd appearance before the jury like this:

Happy was presumably asked to procure girls of the night for Santa Feans, and it was rumored that Sedillo was part of those requesting such services. These parties were typically fueled by a lot of alcohol. . . . Mr. Sedillo came into the grand jury, [but] instead of letting us ask him questions, he read a prepared statement that he was completely innocent of being with Cricket Coogler. (VI)

Based on testimony, the Doña Ana County Grand Jury indicted Sedillo on July 29, 1949. The formal charges against him were (1) giving intoxicating liquor to Cricket Coogler, a minor, at the Bruce Motel in Las Cruces; (2) having Cricket Coogler in his possession for "evil purposes, with the intent of having sexual intercourse with her, and that he remained alone with her in the motel room until after midnight on the night in question, December 7, 1948" (*LCC*, November 10, 1949).

Among the spectators awaiting the announcement of Sedillo's indictment was reporter Walt Finley:

I was being told on one side that Sedillo would not be charged by the Grand Jury and on the other side that Sedillo had been indicted. I wrote the story both ways and submitted both versions. One of my editors published the indictment version, but the first I knew of this is when newsboys outside the courthouse began calling "Extra,

Extra, Sedillo Indicted." I went into the district court and literally got on my knees and prayed that the story was correct. Fortunately it turned out to be so, and the *El Paso Herald Post* had about an eight-hour jump on the story. (VI)

Talking with reporter Walt Finley from his Santa Fe office, Sedillo denied the charges and said that a lot of men had possessed Cricket Coogler for immoral purposes, but that he was singled out for indictment. He said prejudice on the part of the grand jury was the reason for singling him out based solely upon rumor, malice, public clamor, and personal influence. The very wording of his statement that he was "singled out" constituted an admission that he was at least one among those who knew Cricket more than incidentally.

Only a couple of days after his indictments came down, Dan Sedillo was spotted at lunch with state Democratic chair Bryan Johnson at the La Fonda Hotel Restaurant in Santa Fe, a prestigious "in" spot for politicos.

A list of potential jurors in the Third Judicial Court, dated November 9, 1949, shows the notations of the district clerk that eight of twenty-nine possible jurors in the Sedillo case were excused because they had already formed an opinion in the case. The panel finally selected was:

- Robert F. Adams, Las Cruces garageman
- Rudolpho G. Bernal, La Mesa farmer
- Tony Salopek, Mesilla farmer
- William D. Howard, Hatch cannery operator
- Seth G. Acres, Las Cruces grocery employee, foreman
- Donnie Baca, Hatch butcher
- Lowell A. Decker, Las Cruces hardware sales
- R. B. Osborne, White Sands Proving Grounds engineer
- Jack Wareing, Las Cruces
- Joe C. Nevarez, Las Cruces
- Albino M. Gil, Las Cruces
- Fred T. Rivera, Las Cruces

Sedillo's trial began November 9, 1949, in the Las Cruces courtroom of Judge Roy Anderson, Judge William Scoggin having disqualified himself. Dressed in a tan suit, flowered tie, and brown shoes, Sedillo shook hands with many of the courtroom spectators. Sedillo first filed motions for bills of particulars, asking to inspect the testimony transcript and minutes of the grand jury (denied). He also requested specification of the kind of liquor that he allegedly supplied to Cricket Coogler on or about December 7, 1948—whether it was distilled spirits, wine, or beer.

Dan Sedillo's trial attorneys were Harry Bigbee of Santa Fe and Valencia County Democratic chair Filo Sedillo* of Los Lunas (brother to Rufus Sedillo, but no relation to Dan). Attorney Filo Sedillo must have paid particular attention to testimony concerning his brother Rufus, who was said to have been involved in a party December 7, 1948, with Cricket Coogler, Dan Sedillo, Happy Apodaca, and Aurelia McFarland.

Sedillo's attorneys proposed that the indictment be quashed by the court because so many members of the grand jury held personal animosity toward Sedillo, to the extent they became prosecutors, the attorneys claimed, not acting impartially as required by law. The three attorneys also attempted to establish that because Chief Justice Charles Brice was in Roswell, New Mexico, instead of in his seat in Santa Fe, his orders concerning the change in judgeship from Scoggin to Anderson were invalid. That didn't work. Motion denied.

The refusal of the three main witnesses—Happy Apodaca, Rufus Sedillo, and Aurelia McFarland—to answer certain questions brought contempt citations, and the trial was delayed several weeks awaiting the decision of the state supreme court, which finally sided with Bigbee's contention that the contempt citations deprived the witnesses of their liberty. The three were found not guilty of contempt, and the trial proceeded.

Sedillo did not take the stand at any time during his trial, but he had previously denied being in Las Cruces March 30–31, 1949. Although his home was in Las Cruces, he insisted he had not been there since February 26, 1949, when he

> flew to El Paso with Lt. Governor Joe Montoya, and we spent the
> night in Hotel Paso del Norte, before going to Cruces.

---

* Filo Sedillo was a district judge in 1976, according to an October 15, 1976, *Las Cruces Sun-News* story, in which Sedillo directed a verdict of not guilty in the case of Valencia County sheriff Nick Sanchez on charges of converting to his own use a total of $2,739 in jail funds.

I have seen the girl around the Tortugas Café in Las Cruces but I did not know her personally. I can't think who gave the jury my name and I can't imagine what they want of me. (*EPHP*, June 1, 1949)

Even though Joseph "Little Joe" Montoya had visited the city with Sedillo exactly a month before, on February 26, he was not called, and it appeared that no one asked Montoya if he knew Cricket Coogler, or whether he might have accompanied Sedillo again to Las Cruces on March 30.

Dan Sedillo had often denied being in Las Cruces the fateful night. In a weak alibi, he offered documents he said he signed in Santa Fe on March 30 and 31. An employee of his office displayed the documents (*EPHP*, June 1, 1949). Although no one came forward at the time to formally establish that they saw Sedillo in Las Cruces on the night in question, in a late 1990s videotaped interview, Chope Benavides said Dan was "around" that night. And another Las Crucen downtown the night of March 30, 1949, said he personally saw Sedillo that night. A waitress said she served Sedillo dinner on March 30, 1949, and a Las Cruces filling-station operator said he sold Sedillo gasoline the next morning.

The filling-station operator said an automobile of a Santa Fe official was in Las Cruces the morning of March 31. He said he serviced it, and that the Santa Fe man had been drinking. The station was identified as the Corral Service Station on North Main, owned by W. A. Stevens. The local purchase slip was not found, and apparently neither was any record with the companies that honored credit charges to the state via courtesy card no. 13. However, Byron Darden's papers contain a letter from comptroller J. D. Hannah, who wrote that his staff searched through reimbursement vouchers "for the time in question and found none among Dan Sedillo's that shed any light on the matter." Because only Dan Sedillo's vouchers were searched, it is clear enough that these gasoline-purchase questions were about Dan Sedillo.

Cricket's co-worker and friend Katie Etherton had a bit to say about Sedillo:

I do know Dan Sedillo and several others used to come down all the time, and she ran around with them and Happy Apodaca and Joe De Turo.

Later Dan [Sedillo] tried to prove that he was not here, but I personally served Dan Sedillo breakfast at the bus station the next morning. His wife drove down from Santa Fe and picked him up in front of the bus station that Sunday morning. He denied this.

I do know that the night her body was discovered out on the mesa, I was serving drinks at the Elks Club, and Happy was downstairs playing cards when Patrolman [I. E.] Salazar came to tell him the body had been found.

I never did go before the Grand Jury for some reason. . . . I talked to an FBI agent, but somebody blocked me from going to the Grand Jury. (VI)

If Etherton was trying to establish that Dan Sedillo was in town the night of Cricket's disappearance, her above statements cause confusion. March 31, 1949, was a Thursday, not a Sunday. It could make sense that Sedillo's wife, Emelia, might have driven from Santa Fe to pick him up on the Thursday morning of March 31, 1949. The night after Cricket's body was found would have been a Sunday morning weeks later, but it would seem irrelevant and unnecessary to attempt to establish Sedillo's location the day after the body was found.

During Sedillo's trial, two defense attorneys stood at the rear of the court and signaled to the three major witnesses, Happy Apodaca, Aurelia McFarland, and Rufus Sedillo, at points when they should read from a slip of paper their refusal to testify to avoid self-incrimination. Apparently Bigbee did not trust the three to remember the simple language of the Fifth Amendment. "I saw him [Apodaca] pull out of his pocket and try to read the Fifth Amendment," said reporter Alice Gruver, "unable to pronounce some of the words but obviously so proud of himself for not having to testify" (VI). All followed the attorneys' signals correctly except once, when Happy Apodaca read from the slip of paper prematurely, before the question had been asked, and the question was simply whether he had been in Las Cruces on December 7, 1948.

Dan Sedillo never took the stand. In fact, no witnesses were called by the defense.

Cricket's mother, Ollie, dressed in a brown suit with a green scarf, was the first witness for the state. She said Cricket, had she lived, would have been nineteen on November 9 (which had just passed). She denied a story that Cricket had lived at the Herndon Hotel for two months. Rather, she said, Cricket had gone to Florida to visit her [Ollie's] sister for two weeks, and had been gone for a few days or weeks many times. Ollie Coogler also said it was true that when Cricket got off work she often visited bars, against her mother's wishes. When asked if she herself had ever seen Dan Sedillo, Ollie answered no (*EPHP* and *LCC*, November 10, 1949; and *EPT*, November 11, 1949).

Even though the privilege to avoid self-incrimination was used mightily, Judge Anderson overruled a few of the claims to that privilege. He forced a few important answers from assistant state highway engineer Rufus Sedillo. Rufus Sedillo stated that Dan and Cricket stayed at the Bruce Motel while he, Happy, and Aurelia went to the El Patio Bar. When they returned, Rufus said, Apodaca and McFarland took Cricket, who had passed out, to a car. Secondly, Rufus said he never had a date with Cricket, and he did not agree to remove himself from the hotel room so that Dan Sedillo could be alone with her. "I presume they were all drinking," he said. "They were taking shots out of water glasses without any ice or water" (*EPHP*, January 4, 1950). He said a Las Cruces liquor dealer gave state patrolman I. E. Salazar a bottle of liquor, and Salazar in turn gave it to Dan Sedillo. (At least two liquor dealers, Joe De Turo and Freddy Barncastle, were special friends of both Happy Apodaca and Dan Sedillo.) Rufus also confirmed that he and Dan had arrived in Las Cruces about 9:00 p.m. that December night. He said he was on official business in connection with some road work, and Dan came along because "he was interested in some roads and wanted to have a look at them" (*EPHP*, January 4, 1950).

Happy Apodaca was allowed to refuse some questions, but not all.

Question: How long have you known Dan Sedillo?
Apodaca: All my life.
Question: How long have you known Cricket Coogler?
Apodaca (after refusal and overrule): I cannot say.
Question: Did you go any other place with the aforementioned?
Apodaca (after refusal and overrule): To the Patio Café in Old Mesilla.
Question: Did you see Cricket Coogler that night? [December 7, 1948]
Apodaca (after refusal and overrule): Yes.
Question: Did you have any conversation with Dan Sedillo with reference to a date with Cricket?

Apodaca (refusal sustained).

Question: Did you and Aurelia drink together?

Apodaca (after refusal and overrule): We did. (*EPHP*, January 4, 1950)

Apodaca also stated that he did not know where the whiskey he drank that night came from and did not remember who arranged that party (*EPHP*, January 4, 1950).

When it was her turn to be questioned, Aurelia McFarland recounted her version of the events on the evening of December 7, 1948, which she had detailed at Happy Apodaca's removal trial and which supported Rufus Sedillo's testimony. She said she had seen Dan Sedillo, Happy Apodaca, and Rufus Sedillo at the Tortugas Café, where she was working, about 11:00 p.m. on December 7, 1948, and that they all planned to go to Juarez and take Cricket along. They started out for Juarez, but stopped at Freddy Barncastle's Gateway Gardens to dance. Later, she said, they returned to the Bruce Motel, where Dan Sedillo and Cricket stayed in one of the rooms while the rest of the party went to the El Patio bar until it closed around two in the morning. When they returned, she said, Cricket, fully clothed and in a drunken sleep, lay on one bed, and Sedillo, in bedclothes, lay on the other bed. She said she could not remember if she saw either Cricket or Dan drinking whiskey. Throughout Aurelia McFarland's testimony, attorney Harry Bigbee bombarded the court with objections (*EPHP*, January 4, 1950).

Several months earlier, Dan Sedillo had tried another tack in the press. He told Walt Finley he was prepared to refute reports he was with Cricket Coogler a few weeks before her disappearance. He said the man who dated Cricket was another state employee with a name that sounded somewhat like his. This might have pointed a finger toward some other Sedillo, perhaps Rufus or Filo, although one would think Dan would avoid antagonizing either of those Sedillos at the time (*EPHP*, May 28, 1949).

Corinne Massingale, a former Las Cruces waitress, gave a story to Walt Finley that appeared helpful to the prosecution. She said that Cricket Coogler, about three weeks before her death, told how she and another girl had gone to Juarez with a Las Cruces officer and a New Mexico state official. Massingale reported more chilling details supplied by Cricket—namely, that on the way back they stopped at a tourist court, where Cricket said she had been tied to a table, beaten, and raped, although reporters were not clear about who Cricket accused of those things. Massingale supposedly named names only in front of the grand jury, and that testimony remained secret, protected by law. After the incident, Massingale said she asked Cricket about a bruised chin and forehead, and Cricket answered, "That's what I got for going out with a married man" (*EPHP*, May 24, 1949).

Aurelia McFarland's testimony seemed the clearest indictment of Dan Sedillo, but her word apparently did not weigh equally with that of Dan Sedillo, a state official.

In instructions to the jury as they began deliberations, the judge reminded them that the term "possession" meant "either by physical force, persuasion or inducement on the part of the defendant or design by the defendant and intended by him to create a willingness on the part of Ovida Coogler to submit to the control, custody and domination of the defendant" (Archives, Third Judicial District Court Case).

On January 4, 1950, the jury, after only eight hours of deliberation, found Dan Sedillo not guilty. As early as June 7, 1949, he had made a statement reported in the *Las Cruces Sun-News* that in the future, his wife Emelia would accompany him on all trips around the state.

12 Wesley Byrd and the Torture Trial

When Walt Finley heard that as many as fifty people sometimes lined up at the bus station in Las Cruces to get news about the Coogler case from an *El Paso Herald-Post*, he went to see if that was true. Apparently it was.

For many months, Finley practically lived in Las Cruces, following leads about the Coogler case. As the year 1950 began, he was still interviewing people, searching for new information. At that time, he spoke briefly with a waitress at the Tortugas Café/bus station about the case. She gestured toward a black man seated in the café and said that man might know something about it. The man was Wesley Byrd. At first, Byrd was nervous and wouldn't say much, but Finley just kept the coffee coming and kept talking about how long he had been working on this story, and so forth. Finally Wesley Byrd mentioned that he had a story to tell, and Walt Finley listened.

Wesley Byrd, twenty-eight years old, "a Negro" as he was invariably described, was arrested as a suspect soon after Cricket's body was found. It was Wesley Byrd's story that would shed an awful light on Happy Apodaca, Hubert Beasley, and Roy Sandman and send the three of them to federal prison.

Wesley Eugene Byrd was a slender, good-looking, volatile man who was not shy with women. Byrd married Emma Heredia, a Hispanic woman from Madrid, New Mexico. The couple had two children. To marry outside your race was a criminal offense in Texas, and a 1948 arrest for that offense (miscegenation) drove Byrd from El Paso to Las Cruces, where he rented a room. His wife and children stayed in Juarez with her parents. Byrd found a part-time job at the Triple A Garage in Las Cruces, managed by Earl Gentry (Bill Diven, *AJ*, February 23, 1986).

Byrd frequented the Tortugas Café, one of the only Las Cruces diners where a black man could eat in the main dining area. But his flirting with white waitresses bothered the owner of the Tortugas, who complained to Sheriff Happy Apodaca (Diven, *AJ*, February 23, 1986). Since Byrd himself admitted knowing Cricket Coogler when she worked at the Tortugas, it is almost certain she was one of the white waitresses with whom he flirted. However, whether Byrd ever met Cricket Coogler privately on any occasion remained a mystery.

Sheriff Apodaca obviously remembered the complaint from the Tortugas owner and saw Byrd as a possible suspect as he began looking for a solution to the case. Byrd's tendency to flirt with women outside his race had caused him some trouble previously. The FBI obtained a report that while he was overseas in the army during World War II, Byrd reportedly slapped and threw liquor on an Italian girl, and Sheriff Apodaca could have gained access to those records as well.

Byrd's basic military record, excerpted in an FBI report, contained the following:

Inducted	11–17–43 at Fort Bragg, North Carolina
Honorable Discharge as Tech Sergeant	10–31–45, Luzon, Philippine Islands
Re-enlisted	11–1–45, Philippines
General Discharge, Private 1st Class	Sept. 1948, Ft. Bliss, Texas

(Two summary courts martial indicated, one for being off limits and one for violation of curfew) (NARA5)

Understandably, Byrd routinely reported only the honorable discharge (true in 1945, false in 1948), avoiding mention of the less desirable "general" discharge, which describes a discharge under conditions less than honorable. Neither did he dwell on the two courts martial or the loss of his technical sergeant rank. He simply reported his last rank, correctly, as Private First Class. His general truthfulness was to become an important question. Byrd's wife Emma, speaking to an FBI agent, described Byrd as the biggest liar she had ever known.

Someone told FBI agent Henry McConnell that Lonnie Brown, the same schemer who reportedly had in mind setting up Sheriff Apodaca, had also suggested that marijuana could be placed on the person of Wesley Byrd for entrapment purposes, so that Byrd might be arrested. But Byrd was arrested another way, and the gathering of evidence began.

Byrd was picked up for questioning by Deputy Marcelo Hinojosa the afternoon of April 19, 1949, as he sat at Grider's Garage in Las Cruces, where his car was being repaired. Sheriff Happy Apodaca questioned him and, according to Byrd, hit him on the side of the face with a leather strap. The mark was still there when he was released about two weeks later.

Byrd told FBI agents that on April 28, 1949, he was handcuffed and taken on a little trip in the company of Happy Apodaca, state police chief Hubert Beasley, and two state policemen, I. E. "Sally" Salazar and Carlos Salas. Deputy Sheriff Marcelo Hinojosa told the FBI he observed Byrd leaving the courthouse in the company of those four men.

Byrd said he was driven to the site where Cricket Coogler's body had been found, where both a bicycle lock and a padlock were attached to his genitals. The bicycle lock featured two long hasps, with notches along the inside edges. The hasps could be pushed entirely through the base, locking at any serrated position along the way. Byrd was forced to walk with the two locks hanging from him, in excruciating pain, while repeatedly urged to confess to the murder of Cricket Coogler.

The FBI lab received the following evidence from Sheriff Happy Apodaca, along with a cover letter dated April 27, 1949, one day before Byrd was tortured: two cellophane envelopes, one containing some hair ostensibly lifted from Byrd's car and one containing hair from Cricket Coogler's body. In a May 26 response, the lab found that the hairs were similar in color, pigment, diameter, and could be from Cricket Coogler. What makes the hair evidence suspect is that Carl Bamert, Cricket's brother-in-law, disclosed that he visited her desert grave on April 17, the day after the body was found, and discovered some of her hair, which he said he buried about twenty feet from the original grave. The following day, Bamert said Sheriff Apodaca asked to be shown the whereabouts of that hair, and sheriff's deputies took the hair. In a letter to U.S. attorney Ben Brooks, Byron Darden alerted Brooks about the possible planting of Cricket's hair in Byrd's car.

The FBI lab also was asked by Apodaca to examine Cricket's red shoes and reported finding a smear of blue paint on the sole of a shoe. They said it was probably car enamel, which matched the color on Wesley Byrd's dashboard, where paint had been rubbed off in places. The lab could not be certain.

Also examined by the FBI was a sweatshirt of Byrd's with lipstick on it, purported to be the lipstick Cricket Coogler wore. (Cricket's missing purse, which could have contained her lipstick, comes to mind here.) Roy Sandman said he found the sweatshirt in a search at Byrd's address. Wesley Byrd told FBI agents that Sandman had searched his rented room a second time, announcing to Byrd that valuable evidence had been found. Byrd said he had not given permission for such a search.

Byrd had been held for about a week, denied an attorney, before some of his friends missed seeing him around. His landlord mentioned to friends at the U-Totem Grocery that Byrd's room had been turned upside down. Friends Cleo McCarroll, Jasper Williams, Jones Caraway, and Cedric Bradford, proprietor of the U-Totem, read in the paper that a person was being held and went downtown to inquire whether it might be Byrd. The clerk on duty stepped back into the sheriff's private office for a moment, and then returned with the statement that no one by that name was in custody.

Byrd's friends from the U-Totem Grocery, all of whom later made statements to FBI investigators, persisted. They went to attorney W. L. Sullivan, who was able to report that Byrd was indeed being held in jail.

Finally Byrd was charged with selling a car without a dealer's license, but the paper complaint was lost. Several people were involved in the custody of that record. Among them were the district clerk, Byron Darden, LaFel Oman, T. K. Campbell, and his assistant E. E. Chavez (NARA3). Byrd was offered release on a $500 bond, and his friends raised the cash and signed the papers. They described Byrd to FBI agents as quite low in spirits. Byrd had been told at some point that if he confessed, he would be given some money and put across the border (NARA3). At another time, he said he had been told that if he confessed, he would not receive a sentence of more than a year or two (*SFNM*, September 19, 1950). Although those few friends did come to Byrd's aid, they acknowledged that Byrd was not always too accurate in his statements. As they left the jail, they asked Byrd what had happened, but warned him to tell the truth, as if they were aware of a propensity for storytelling (NARA3). Byrd described to his friends in detail the ordeal he had endured.

Soon after his release, Byrd was interviewed by reporter Walt Finley in the Tortugas Café. As Byrd was talking, who should enter the café but patrolman Carlos Salas. Byrd quietly pointed out Patrolman Salas to Finley, saying that Salas did not take part in the torture but was there when it happened.

In May 1949 Byrd sought medical attention and found a job for about a month at Central School before returning to his home in Altapass, North Carolina. One would imagine he could not leave Las Cruces fast enough, but he may have had no choice except to work in the town a few weeks to earn enough for the trip home. Of course, he had to return for the torture trial in 1950, but he would not enter New Mexico again.

This publicity, and the FBI lab's examination of evidence in the case, caught the interest of FBI director J. Edgar Hoover. Hoover was especially sensitive to stories about violations of human and civil rights at the time, because his FBI was being criticized for failing to find persons responsible for bombings and lynchings in the South. Perhaps an additional impetus for J. Edgar Hoover's special interest in the Byrd case was simply some words from Governor Mechem, a former FBI agent himself. Hoover was said to have prided himself on knowing each of his agents personally.

The reports of FBI investigators were presented to a federal grand jury in Santa Fe. The twenty-one all-male federal grand jury members heard several cases over the years 1949 and 1950. Twelve votes were required to return an indictment. The jury members were:

- Milas Hurley, Tucumcari, foreman
- Dan Taichert, Santa Fe, deputy foreman
- Charles McCulley, Albuquerque
- Jim Mahill, Mayhill
- Blas R. Ortega, El Porvenir
- Tomas J. Martinez, Mora
- Will Shuster, Santa Fe
- Tobias Espinosa, Tierra Amarilla
- William L. Erb, Las Vegas
- Paul Davis, Milnesand

- William Bamberger, Magdalena
- W. J. Clemens, Santa Fe
- Celso Turrietta, Albuquerque
- Camilo Medina, Alcalde
- Vance N. West, Albuquerque
- Herman Fitzner, Logan
- Cleto Gallegos, El Porvenir
- Seale Howe, Wagon Mound
- J. P. Abbin, Albuquerque
- Charles Alford, Causey
- Elmer Burnett, Bellview

In July this federal grand jury issued four warrants of arrest regarding the Coogler case, charging participation in the torture of Wesley Byrd in order to coerce a confession to her murder. Sheriff Happy Apodaca, police chief Hubert Beasley, deputy Roy Sandman, and patrolman I. E. "Sally" Salazar were indicted on two counts: (1) conspiracy to violate civil rights of another, and (2) actual deprivation of those civil rights.* I. E. "Sally" Salazar and Carlos Salas were summoned from their respective 1950 posts at Carrizozo and Chama.

Just before he was served the warrant, Happy Apodaca, working as a carpenter at a Fort Bliss housing project at the time, commented that he knew only what he had read in the newspapers about the torture. He said:

At no time while I was sheriff of Doña Ana County have I been guilty of such charges.

During my term in office no such offenses were committed by Roy Sandman or any other deputy in my office, Chief Beasley or any state patrolman, to my knowledge. (*EPHP*, July 13, 1950)

---

* It is noteworthy that at the end of September 1950, after all the charges and the trial having to do with the torture of Wesley Byrd were complete, the federal grand jury was reconvened. Cedric Bradford, the same twenty-eight-year-old grocer from Las Cruces who noticed Byrd's absence from his U-Totem Grocery, was named foreman—the first black foreman of a federal grand jury in the United States.

The Torture Trial

Santa Fe, New Mexico, September 18–22, 1950

The trial of Happy Apodaca, Hubert Beasley, Roy Sandman, and I. E. "Sally" Salazar began September 18, 1950, before federal judge Carl Hatch in Santa Fe. The case, numbered 15982, was quickly commonly referred to in New Mexico as "The Torture Trial." The special government prosecutor was Ben Brooks, who had recently accomplished the convictions of a Dallas sheriff, two Alabama policemen, and a Mississippi officer for violations of the civil rights of Negro prisoners.

The attorneys for the defendants were H. A. Kiker of Santa Fe for Hubert Beasley, "Bantam Rooster" Bigbee for both Apodaca and Salazar, and former New Mexico governor A. T. Hannett of Albuquerque for Sandman.

Juror Carl Crutchfield's upset stomach caused a one-hour delay in the opening of the trial, and alternate juror Otniel Lopez had been summoned just in case. However, Lopez failed to answer the jury summons right away, because his car had overturned en route to Santa Fe. Finally, however, the following jury was in place:

- Marvin E. Powell, Lovington farmer
- Claudio Aragon, Colfax County rancher
- James Nuckols, Roosevelt County rancher
- Carl Crutchfield, Lovington credit manager (Otniel Lopez, alternate)
- John S. Shearman, Artesia barber
- Stephen L. Block, Harding County rancher
- Max J. Salazar, Wagon Mound merchant
- Howard Martin, Clovis
- Earl Grau, Tucumcari
- W. W. Doran, Hobbs auto dealer
- Max Fernandez, Taos County merchant
- Ralph Becker, Albuquerque banker

According to Cedric Bradford, who attended the trial, the attorneys for the defendants were stymied by Wesley Byrd, who remained calm and unshaken throughout the trial, answering questions articulately, refusing to be danced into any position he did not wish to take (AI). According to FBI special agent Henry McConnell, attorney LaFel Oman had advised Byrd's lawyers that Byrd was "far from humble" and should be cautioned to answer precisely, not go beyond the scope of the question, and further, to exhibit as nearly as possible a dignified and restrained bearing (NARA1). Byrd seemed to take that advice.

Cedric Bradford also observed that one of the attorneys for the defense used the word "nigger" over and over, until Judge Hatch called the whole defense-attorney group to the bench to admonish them for it. The word was not heard again in that courtroom (AI).

Byrd, of course, gave extensive testimony. However, his testimony was simply mentioned within coverage of policeman Carlos Salas's testimony, and Byrd's name was rarely featured in a headline. A typical headline read: "Officer Supports Negro's Testimony in Torture Case," wording that was typical at the time.

Byrd said that on the way to the torture site, he waited alone in the car as the lawmen stopped for cigarettes and liquor. In their absence, he said he shouted to someone in the vicinity that he was being taken out to be killed. No one could be found to confirm this story. Byrd also said he smelled whiskey on both Beasley and Apodaca when they returned to the car, and that he had already smelled whiskey on both men before the stop.

Byrd said Sheriff Apodaca told him he was being taken on a one-way ride. When they arrived at the desert site, one of the deputies pointed to a mesquite bush and identified it as Cricket's gravesite. Byrd told *Sun-News* reporter O. E. Rouse that he was made to actually lie down in the grave as they pointed guns at him.

Byrd described his arrest and the torture trip.

One of Sheriff Happy Apodaca's men came in and greeted me in Spanish. I answered the greeting in Spanish. He told me the high sheriff wanted to see me at the county courthouse. . . . They questioned me [over twelve days and then] several deputies took me out of my cell, put me in a car, and drove to a spot near an old cemetery.

The deputy put a metal clamp on me and told me to admit I killed Cricket. I told him I didn't kill the girl. He told me they had examined my car and that they had found some of Miss Coogler's hair in the back seat. He told me if I didn't confess he would shoot me and bury me where I buried Cricket. (*EPHP*, May 10, 1949)

Byrd described to FBI agents more graphically what he meant by "a metal clamp":

> Apodaca took a small lock from the glove compartment of his car and then he and Beasley tried to force the lock around my penis and testicles which Apodaca had taken out of my trousers [as Byrd was handcuffed]. The lock was so small they were unable to accomplish this. . . . Apodaca said he would go get something that would make me talk. . . . (NARA1) [Apodaca reportedly left with Salazar, returned with a larger lock and Roy Sandman as a passenger.]
>
> Apodaca removed from his pocket a new bicycle lock. . . . Apodaca and Beasley then placed the bicycle lock around my penis and part of my testicles and locked it as tight as they could get it . . . then took a part of my testicles and fastened the other small lock tight around it. . . . Apodaca said he would remove the locks if I would confess the murder. I told him I would die first. (NARA1)
>
> I . . . wasn't going to take the blame for something I didn't do. I asked him [unclear whether this was Beasley or Apodaca] not to torture me any more. He cursed me. Then they drove me back to the jail and locked me up. Four days later they charged me with selling a car without a dealer's license. I can't understand that charge. It was my own car. . . . I was in perfect condition when I got out of the Army a few months ago. [Now] I'm undergoing medical treatment and I may have to have an operation. (*EPHP*, May 10, 1949)

Byrd also quoted Hubert Beasley's remark that if he (Byrd) were the type of fellow his wife said he was, a padlock put around his balls would be too good for him (Brief of Beasley Appeal, DP).

"The officers were laughing," Byrd said. "I told them they could shoot me, but I wasn't taking another step" (Unnumbered transcript of Byrd interview, NARA). Descriptions of how much time was spent in the desert varied from a couple of hours, according to Sandman, who might have underestimated, to three and a half hours, according to Byrd, who might have understandably overestimated.

Byrd said two jailers told him they had been ordered not to give him medical aid when he was returned, although he was in great pain and suffering severe nausea. Attorney Harry Bigbee offered a motion that Byrd be given another physical examination by a doctor selected by the defense, who could supposedly confirm that no such torture occurred, because (1) permanent injury would have necessarily resulted if Byrd had been telling the truth, and (2) large bicycle-type padlocks could not be used in the manner described (*EPHP*, September 19, 1950). The motion was denied by Judge Hatch, and the jury seemed able to visualize the method described.

Dr. George Leonard, Veterans Administration physician in El Paso, had examined Byrd soon after his release from jail. In a memo to the FBI, the doctor said Byrd was swollen and tender and showed a line of irritation, or what might be called a welt, at the upper part of his scrotum as if a ligature had been applied. His patient told him he had been kidnapped and taken out into the desert and tortured in order to make him confess to a crime, but Dr. Leonard thought the tale so fantastic he did not make official entry of it. However, neither did he forget the incident (NARA3).

Byrd's friend Jones Caraway said that he observed Byrd leaving the county jail, walking "spraddle-legged like he was sore" (*SFNM*, September 19, 1950). Caraway offered to demonstrate in the courtroom exactly how Wesley Byrd was walking, but Judge Hatch ruled that unnecessary.

Byrd's part-time employer, Earl Gentry, manager of the Triple A Garage in Las Cruces, told FBI agents that Byrd showed him the bruises on his scrotum and told him how they happened. Gentry said the Triple A Garage handled contracts for the Doña Ana County Sheriff's Office at the time, and he was forced to fire Wesley Byrd through pressure by Sheriff Apodaca, who allegedly threatened to deprive the garage of contract business from the sheriff's office, as well as the New Mexico Highway Patrol (NARA1). Gentry himself was living in Oxford, Mississippi, by November 1949—not the first who suddenly felt unwelcome in Las Cruces.

More damning testimony at the trial came from FBI agent William Damon, who said Apodaca showed him a bicycle lock and described its use on a Negro suspect in the Coogler case. Agent Damon filed a report saying Apodaca had talked to him in front of the Tortugas Café on April 28, 1949, the very date of Byrd's torture, about ten o'clock in the evening, inviting Damon to come to his office the following day so he could show him something. On the following morning, Damon reminded Apodaca of this, and Apodaca unlocked his desk, removed a large bicycle lock, and told Damon he and Beasley had used it on a Negro suspect he believed was guilty but who would not confess. Apodaca illustrated to Damon how tight the lock had been squeezed by leaving a space at the top of the hasp of approximately two inches (NARA1).

Merchant Joe E. Viramontes Jr. testified that in late April 1949 he sold Apodaca a bicycle padlock like the one described. Viramontes said that after purchasing the lock, Apodaca traveled south toward El Paso. On cross-examination, Viramontes said Apodaca had bought a bicycle from him as well, the Christmas before (*SFNM*, September 20, 1950). In what must have been a chilling moment at the trial, Wesley Byrd said that he saw Apodaca put a padlock in a car door pocket as they left the jail (*LCSN*, September 19, 1950). He did not say whether he thought nothing of it at the time or anticipated its purpose.

Byrd testified that Apodaca, Beasley, and Sandman had each struck him once at some point during his incarceration. Sandman said in denial: "The only time that I touched him was upon interrogation when he jumped out of his chair, swinging his arms, and I pushed him back in the chair and handcuffed his hands around the arm rest of the chair to prevent him from striking me. I did not hit him; I merely shoved him back in the chair" (*EPHP*, July 13, 1950). Deputy Marcelo Hinojosa recounted to FBI agents his observation of that scene, recalling Byrd's comment that Sandman might keep him in jail, dry him up, or starve him, but someday "I'll get out." Sandman asked, "Then what?" Byrd did not answer for a bit, then smiled and said, "Then *I'll* go back home." From the way Byrd said it, Hinojosa said he gained the impression that Byrd was threatening harm to Sandman (NARA1). The night jailer, Augustine Madrid, told FBI agents that a very angry Byrd called deputy Roy Sandman "white trash" during one interview, and Sandman said Byrd spat at his face (NARA3).

I. E. "Sally" Salazar had a legitimate reason to leave the torture scene. Although he did not testify at the torture trial, he told FBI agents that while at the desert site, he remembered that his presence was necessary at a hearing at the courthouse before justice of the peace Jack Robertson, so Apodaca drove him back to town. He hurried to the courtroom of Justice Robertson, who was just announcing that the hearing was postponed to a later date. Salazar said he returned to Coogler's desert gravesite, alone this time, in a separate police vehicle. Judge Robertson said his court records supported Salazar's story (NARA1).

Roy Sandman did not go out to the desert gravesite with the initial group, but he joined them later by riding out with Apodaca after I. E. Salazar had been delivered to his court appointment. Sandman denied any abuse, or even seeing any padlocks of any kind.

Police chief Beasley, in his appeal brief and elsewhere, contended that the long bicycle lock Apodaca retrieved on the short trip to town was intended only as a visible threat, and that there was no torture (DP).

It seems that the day Byrd was taken to Cricket's desert grave, he did not yet know who state police chief Beasley was, referring to Beasley initially as "one of the deputies" (*SFNM*, September 21, 1950). And, remarkably, Byrd alleged no mistreatment by Roy Sandman or Sally Salazar at the desert gravesite, except to say that they held him as Apodaca and Beasley applied the locks (NARA1).

When special agent Henry McConnell attempted to interview Happy Apodaca concerning the treatment of Byrd, Apodaca declined to comment.

Then all eyes at the trial fell on Emma Heredia, the estranged wife of Wesley Byrd, who was present in the Santa Fe courtroom, described as "childlike, of slight stature, wearing a green dress and spike-heeled shoes." Attorney Kiker asked Byrd if it was true that he married a white girl. "No sir," said Byrd. "Didn't you marry one of our New Mexico Spanish-blooded girls?" Kiker persisted. "No, she was from Old Mexico," Byrd said (*SFNM*, September 19, 1950). Byrd mentioned to the FBI that Sheriff Apodaca had shown "a great deal of interest in the fact that I had married a Spanish girl" (NARA1).

Emma Heredia recalled talking with Sheriff Happy Apodaca twice: once when he arrived at her Juarez, Mexico, home and gave her bus money so that she could appear in his office the following day, and then in his office the following day, where the sheriff himself typed a statement in his private office, read it aloud to Emma, and obtained her signature. Emma did not herself read the statement, only listened as Apodaca read it. It was not established whether or not she read English, only that she could speak some of it. She invariably requested conversations in Spanish, which the sheriff provided. Emma was emphatic that the statement was correct as read aloud to her, and she willingly signed it. This statement, which the FBI located in the files of state police chief Hubert Beasley, appeared as follows:

Date 4-28-49

I, Emma Heredia states [*sic*] that Wesley Byrd was not in my mother's house in Juarez, Mexico on Wed. [*sic*] March 30th 1949, because that day I was home, I remember that the last time he was over at my mother's home was the time that he took my brother-in-law to the Hospital . . . [sometime before] the 6th day of March 1949. The last time that I saw Wesley Byrd was sometime in the month of February 1949, but I don't remember the date, and it was in El Paso, Texas in the Canton Café, but I didn't talk to him then, soon as he came in I walked out.

I married Wesley Byrd in Las Cruces, New Mexico on May 29th 1948, and every [*sic*] since then, he had treated me very bad, all he wanted me for was for sexual purposes, because it looked to me that he wanted to have sexual intercourse all the time, I know from my own mind that he is a sex maniac, and that he would not stop at nothing [*sic*] if he didn't get what he wanted. That's the main reason that I left him, because I know that some time or other he would get mad at me and that he would harm me, and the sooner I would get away from him the better it would be for me. . . . He get what he want [*sic*] at any price. I don't know why Sheriff Apodaca is asking me all this questions [*sic*], but maybe because he wants to know something about Wesley Byrd's conduct, and what I have told Sheriff Apodaca is the truth and nothing but the truth. Signed Emma Heredia. (NARA1)

Emma's statement was signed on the very day established as the day Wesley Byrd was tortured, April 28, 1949. In fact, she said Apodaca commented to her at the beginning of their meeting that they had just brought Byrd in. Emma, of course, could not realize what that meant or where Byrd had been taken.

Deputy Roy Sandman, who was called in to witness Emma's signature on the statement, told an FBI agent he did not speak Spanish but observed Emma to be in a cooperative mood. He said he did not participate in the interview, nor did he observe the preparation of her statement. No one could say whether Sheriff Apodaca added or subtracted any wording in his verbal rendition of the statement to Emma. The phrasing and diction, at least, seems most inconsistent: "He get what he want" indicates a person having more trouble with English than one who in the next breath can use this sentence: "[M]aybe he wants to know something about Wesley Byrd's conduct." The possibility that the wording was not Emma's, but Apodaca's, exists.

Emma said she had not lived with Byrd for five months preceding his arrest. When questioned as to the sexual details of the statement, Emma's only reply was that Wesley really loved her. FBI special agent McConnell said it could not be determined whether Emma was reluctant to discuss the allegation that Byrd had married her for "sexual purposes," or whether it was impossible to make her understand the nature of the questions. She also called Byrd "crazy," but McConnell said it was again impossible to induce her to say how or why. She did offer one story about Byrd's lying. She said he once appeared at her mother's Juarez address saying Emma had been in an automobile accident and was in a hospital in El Paso in critical condition. Emma said she was right there in the home, and her mother was aware of her whereabouts and her physical condition (NARA1).

Emma repeated positively that she had not seen Byrd in March or April of 1949, but said someone had knocked vigorously on her mother's front door early one morning in April and her mother observed from the window that it was Wesley Byrd. He left when no one answered the door (NARA1). With "one morning in April" such a vague date, Wesley Byrd could have been in Juarez March 31–April 1, 1949.

Emma's former employer, Jim Day, who had a small restaurant on Las Cruces Street, told Agent McConnell that Emma was afraid of her husband, and that he (Day) had felt forced to intervene one day when Byrd came in shouting his objection to Emma's working there. He said Byrd refused to leave until he was chased out the back door. Then Emma took twelve dollars with Day's permission and left immediately. Some days later, upon opening his shop, Day found an envelope under the front door with twelve dollars in it. Although it contained no markings, he was confident it was from Emma.

Day also told Agent McConnell about another episode, a story that could not have been more tailored to justify Apodaca's arrest of Byrd. Although Day could not place the date, he said Emma told him that shortly before Cricket Coogler's disappearance, Byrd, drunk, attempted to convince Emma to get into a car with him and a Tortugas Café waitress named Mary. Emma refused because of Byrd's condition, and because she saw blood and hair in Byrd's car. When questioned closely about this statement attributed to her, Emma repeated only that she had not seen Byrd at any time (although her mother had) during the months of March or April 1949 (NARA1). The vague date was the key, since any blood or hair in Byrd's car at any time prior to the night of March 30, 1949, would not have offered any evidence about Cricket Coogler's death.

In November 1949 Emma's mother, Dolores Heredia, was interviewed by FBI agents McConnell and Rousseau. She was very worried because she had not seen nor heard from Emma for a month and a half, since the day Emma told her she was running away in fear of Byrd. Dolores Heredia remembered severe bruises on Emma's throat and arms, which Emma said were the result of Wesley Byrd's actions, but Dolores did not connect a date to these bruises. She said Emma had been working at a Mesilla Park (a Las Cruces suburb) beauty shop. But Mesilla Park apparently had no beauty shop, and the only one in Old Mesilla, the nearby historic village, was in the rear of the Economy Store and had employed no one of Emma's name or description (NARA3). Vague reports did later surface that Emma was working in El Paso, and then that she was somewhere on the West Coast.

As to the night of Cricket's disappearance, Byrd claimed in a statement to the FBI, and presumably at the trial as well, that he was in Juarez (although he said he was not certain of the date) at the Rex Bar with friends Johnny Lurias and "B" Lucas, Fort Bliss soldiers, who then drove Byrd to a Juarez hotel about five blocks south, the name of which Byrd said he could not pronounce in Spanish. Byrd stated that on April 1 he again met the two friends about 11:00 a.m. at the Rex Bar, after which they drove him to Fort Bliss to look at a black 1935 Buick sedan with a loose rod. They ate at the Company B mess hall, where Byrd went back to the kitchen to visit some of the friends with whom he used to cook (Unnumbered transcript of Byrd interview, NARA).

Police chief Hubert Beasley continually maintained that Byrd was not touched or harmed in his presence. It would have been Wesley Byrd's word against Apodaca's, Beasley's and Sandman's, except that one important person backed up Byrd's story: patrolman Carlos Salas. At the Torture Trial, Salas became the star witness by saying straight out that he had seen Beasley place the first of two padlocks on Wesley Byrd. He said he saw the second padlock on Byrd but did not know who applied that one (*EPHP*,

September 19, 1950). Salas had given this same account, matching well with Byrd's, to an FBI confidential informant called T-1 (NARA1).

Salas admitted that he had wrongly told the county grand jury that nothing unusual had occurred in the treatment of Byrd, but had done so because he was trying to protect himself. "I was present when these things were happening and I thought I was involved," Salas said. "There wasn't a lawyer in Las Cruces I could talk to." Salas said he was sickened by what was happening to Byrd and walked away a good distance, pretending to look for clothing of Cricket Coogler, because he could not "stand to see what was going on" (*SFNM*, September 19, 1950). Carlos Salas also confirmed that Apodaca and Salazar were indeed gone for about an hour from the torture scene, and when they returned, Apodaca brought Sandman in his car, and Salazar drove a second car.

It was most likely Carlos Salas's testimony that clinched the convictions, especially that of police chief Beasley. Salas, of course, must have feared for his job and his family, but nevertheless he gave his account of what occurred.

Some bad blood simmered in the background between state police chief Hubert Beasley and patrolman Carlos Salas. Carlos Salas's public profile in Doña Ana County was similar to Sheriff Happy Apodaca's, along with a varied reputation ranging from fairness to arrogance and intimidating ways. In November 1949 Beasley had been charged with assault and battery when he allegedly struck Salas at a dance in Carlsbad following Beasley's election as president of the Sheriffs and Police Association at their annual convention (*LCC*, November 3, 1949). (Two years later, the same association unanimously refused to accept Beasley's proffered resignation following his conviction in the Byrd case [*SFNM*, October 4, 1950].)

News editor Homer Gruver observed:

I have a hunch there's some bad feeling between Beasley and Salas. Salas—and Patrolman I. E. Salazar—were the two who testified at Apodaca's Silver City trial that the reason they had not raided gambling in the lower valley was that Beasley had ordered them to keep hands-off. That testimony, apparently, was the reason Patrolman Salazar was assigned to Vaughn, N.M., considered by the state police as the least desirable place in the state to be stationed. The weather there in the winter time is atrocious. (*LCC*, November 9, 1949)

Chief Beasley denied he had issued any such orders to banish Salazar. But with bad blood between Salas and Beasley already simmering, Salas's straightforward testimony was enough to burn the pan. In May 1951, the new state police chief, Joe Roach, transferred Carlos Salas to Carrizozo, about halfway between Las Cruces and Vaughan. Salas's request for a hearing on the transfer was denied (*LCSN*, May 14 and 15, 1951).

Defendants Happy Apodaca and I. E. Salazar did not testify at the torture trial.

Salazar had declared to FBI interviewers that the stop on the way out to Mesquite was made only for cigarettes, and that no member of the party took a drink of any alcoholic beverage in his presence. Byrd said that Sheriff Apodaca did give him a pack of cigarettes when the group returned to the car (NARA2). This might seem astounding unless one had some experience with Sheriff Happy Apodaca.

Because Salazar returned to the torture site some vague time after Apodaca and Sandman, it is possible he was late enough to miss some of the torture; but Byrd told the FBI he remembered that Salazar arrived alone in a police car *about the same time* as Apodaca and Sandman. If that were the case, the bicycle lock had just arrived, the torture was far from over, and Salazar had to see it. Nevertheless, that little trip back to town saved Sally Salazar.

Judge Hatch gave the jury fifty-seven minutes of instruction, and the jury finally began to deliberate at 9:16 p.m. on September 20, 1950. As usual, no proceeding went smoothly in any case related to Cricket Coogler's death. The verdicts were returned only after federal judge Carl Hatch twice sent the jury back to work after it was unable to come to any agreement. After several sessions stretching as long as eleven hours, the jury in Santa Fe gave Wesley Byrd a taste of justice. They voted to convict Happy Apodaca of violation of civil rights and conspiracy to violate the civil rights of Wesley Byrd. They voted to convict Hubert Beasley of violation of those same civil rights. They voted to convict Roy Sandman on the conspiracy count only—likely as a result of Byrd's and Carlos Salas's testimony that Sandman was not present at the torture initially.

Sally Salazar was exonerated, although Wesley Byrd said that Salazar did beat him upon the hands with something hard whenever he tried to protect himself. (Incidentally, Salazar's bond money had been put up by Emelia Sedillo, Dan's wife, according to notes in author Tony Hillerman's archived papers.)

Byrd confirmed that Carlos Salas, who was never charged, apparently had not participated in the torture, having removed himself as far away from the awful scene as he could. Byrd said Salas did approach him near the end of the ordeal to advise him to tell the truth so he would not be hurt any more. "I was so sick I didn't even answer," Byrd said in a statement in FBI files. "They put me back in the car. They saw I was very sick and stopped at a store near Mesquite, gave me two orange soda pops. I was very thirsty" (Unnumbered transcript of Byrd interview, NARA). It is easy to imagine the humiliation and rage Byrd must have felt on the way back to the jail, although his handcuffs were removed so that he could hold the drink himself.

Pronounced guilty, the three defendants appealed to the U.S. Circuit Court for a reversal of their convictions, but the appeal failed. The next step would have been the U.S. Supreme Court, which had handed down a decision against just such an appeal the previous week, which would have been a terribly expensive undertaking. The defendants waited out the obligatory twenty days to file an appeal, did not do so, and were taken into custody.

Hubert Beasley, age forty-eight; Roy Sandman, fifty-two; and Happy Apodaca, thirty-seven, began their prison sentences only a few days apart in the middle of June 1951. Both Apodaca and Beasley asked for reduced sentences, claiming hardship on their families and impaired health, but Judge Carl Hatch said no. Happy Apodaca did not go quietly. He arrived in Las Cruces from Garfield, where he had been working on the family farm, one night in advance, and spent most of the night talking to friends in Las Cruces bars. The next day, as Apodaca awaited his escort to La Tuna Federal Detention Farm near El Paso, Texas, Walt Finley recorded a few of Apodaca's statements:

The day Cricket's body was found down there in the sandhills near Mesquite, I tried to get in touch with Campbell. I couldn't. I couldn't get in touch with him until the next day. Then he asked me what investigation I had made. I told him. He thought it was all right. Yet, I'm the guy in trouble.

It wasn't my idea to put that lock on Byrd. [Here he was pointing out that Beasley had been in charge.]

Yes, I'm going to prison, the man who was the most popular man in Doña Ana County three years ago is going to prison. I used to get more votes than anybody. Don't think I'm not still popular. I am. I could be elected for office again. But I'm not going to run again. Not me. I'm through with law enforcement work.

When I get out of La Tuna, I'll make some kind of a success.

I have been kicked around plenty about the Cricket Coogler case. I was right, but no one would believe me. I arrested Jerry Nuzum. Tommy Campbell, the district attorney, turned him loose. Now Nuzum has been arrested again and will be tried for murder.

Why did I turn him loose? I asked Campbell for three days to file a murder charge against Nuzum. He wouldn't do it. He turned Nuzum loose.

I also told Campbell I was going to issue a statement about gossip about me and Cricket. Campbell advised me not to. He said it would only place me on the defensive. (*EPHP*, June 14, 1951)

Apodaca blamed T. K. Campbell for mishandling Nuzum's case. Because Campbell hired Roy Sandman away from Apodaca, as well as other conflicts that likely arose during the investigations, Apodaca and Campbell probably were not on good terms in the summer of 1951.

Roy Sandman had a bit to say on his way to prison: "I could tell a lot if I wanted to. This thing has only started" (*EPHP*, June 14, 1951). He declined to explain further what he meant, and he was dead soon after he was released from prison, before follow-up questions could be satisfied. His death was ruled a suicide, a ruling with which his family disagreed.

None of the three convicted men, because of their status as federal prisoners, were allowed visitors at La Tuna Federal Detention Farm, but each served less than their one-year sentences. Apodaca and Sandman served ten months, each doing some cooking in the prison mess. Beasley, who swept the prison administration building and did other janitorial work, served nine months. Walt Finley said that Happy Apodaca, while in prison, had the bad judgment to address a letter to one of Apodaca's brothers, telling him in so many words, "You know if you knock off this family, I'll have the perfect alibi" (VI). The FBI seized the letter. Which family was indicated remains a mystery, and Apodaca likely insisted this was a joke.

One of many unanswered questions is whether Apodaca might have been contacted from a powerful office and directed in no uncertain terms that, failing to coerce a confession from Byrd, he had better see to it that *somebody* was framed. Allegedly, Byrd was not the only target of a frame. Two other men claimed to have been beaten in order to coerce their confessions to the murder of Cricket Coogler: Lauren Welch and William Conaway.

Lauren Welch, one of Cricket's boyfriends, reported that he had been mistreated, hit by a local state policeman during questioning about the Coogler case, even made to strip at one point. When asked whether the state policeman was Carlos Salas or Sally Salazar, the only two assigned to Doña Ana County, he said it was the bigger man. That would have been Salazar. When asked if he had made any complaint about this, Welch commented that he was going to "get these guys in his own time and way" (NARA1).

An FBI report also recounts the story of a White Sands Proving Grounds civilian employee, William Conaway, who said he was picked up in downtown Las Cruces by sheriff's deputies and questioned about Cricket Coogler. He said highway patrolman Salazar, Sheriff Apodaca, and Deputy Sandman strapped him to a chair, wrapped his head with towels, and beat him when he told them he never heard of her. He had just moved to Las Cruces from Muleshoe, Texas, the day he was picked up. He was released from custody with no charges filed. Pictures were allegedly made of Conaway's battered face at El Chico Studio in Las Cruces, and White Sands officials were said to be in possession of those pictures. When officers went to the studio and demanded the pictures or negatives, El Chico employees failed to find them (*EPHP*, May 27, 1949). Conaway was not named again in connection to the case.

Speculation continued in endless waves over the long and hot summer of 1950. On one of those hot July evenings, a bit of vigilantism disturbed the Doña Ana County Sheriff's Office, now headed by Jose Viramontes. About 10:30 on the evening of July 12, those inside heard a loud cracking noise, after which they found a small, round gunshot hole in one of the window panes.

Other news crowded onto the front pages in mid-1951. President Harry Truman fired General Douglas MacArthur, who arrived in Washington to defend himself in an address to the U.S. Congress. MacArthur was given a wild welcome in New York City, where an astonishing seven and a half million persons turned out to welcome him, and vessels in the harbor tied down their whistles for continuous noise to add to the din. Happy Apodaca, Hubert Beasley, and Roy Sandman now followed such local and national news from their new location, La Tuna Federal Detention Farm, just across the Texas line.

The *Las Cruces Sun-News* featured advertisements of interest to women in Doña Ana County: White's Auto in downtown Las Cruces featured a new crescent-style mohair sofa with a fringed base. The price for it and its matching chair was $359: $39 down and $5.25 a week. A feature story gave the results of a study that showed that U.S. males spent an average of $167 for an engagement ring. Other women may have been dreaming about how such ads might affect their lives, but the time for that had passed for Cricket Coogler.

Cricket had been dead for almost two hectic, confusing years. She was still a favorite topic of discussion in cafés, especially in those where patrons could easily still remember the sound of her high heels approaching their table and a quick-witted comment behind a little, defiant smile.

A game of cards provides an analogy for building theories about the Cricket Coogler case, if each card represents a person and can be grouped and regrouped in hundreds of ways. The cards are not of equal value: some are twos and threes; some are kings and aces. The order in which cards are played is an individual decision. Cricket Coogler's death may have been a chance accident. One card, one man, could have accomplished her death alone; a pair of men, perhaps three, could have worked together; and so forth. To complicate the exercise, one is never sure the full deck of cards has ever been laid on the table.

Some of the men listed alphabetically below were questioned as suspects. Others may have been knowledgeable about some elements of the case, innocent observers, or the subject of pure, unfair gossip. Some were even doing what they could to solve the case. A couple of these names have scarcely been mentioned in previous chapters. Nevertheless, each carries some potential as an interesting subject if he could be interviewed today, as detailed in the bulleted statements.

Happy Apodaca

- Doña Ana County sheriff Happy Apodaca was found guilty of torturing Wesley Byrd to coerce a confession to the murder of Cricket

Coogler. Two other men said they were also roughly treated by Apodaca and asked to confess to her murder.

- Apodaca delayed the search for Cricket Coogler for five days.
- When summoned to the site where Cricket Coogler's body lay, Apodaca appeared nervous.
- Apodaca took Cricket Coogler home on several occasions and was well acquainted with her.
- Apodaca often drank too much and could be violent. Examples: the alleged rapes/attempted rapes, his armed and drunken threat to reporter Walt Finley, and violence against Wesley Byrd, Corporal Willie Cahoon, Dan Williams, and others. (It was Williams's broken jaw and displaced eye that resulted in Apodaca's release from the state police force.)
- According to Aurelia McFarland, Apodaca was in Las Cruces in the early morning hours of March 31, 1949, since he did not leave for Albuquerque until later that morning.
- Ollie Coogler, Cricket's mother, told attorney Byron Darden that Sheriff Apodaca had mentioned to her that he saw Cricket on March 30.
- Apodaca was named by FBI informants as one who took payoff money from illegal gambling establishments.
- Apodaca was regarded as a womanizer at best, a serial rapist at worst.
- Apodaca was named by one source as the father of a baby Cricket was supposedly carrying.
- Apodaca, although new to his job as sheriff, was familiar with county roads.
- An unidentified person told attorney Byron Darden that Apodaca was "always borrowing a car."
- According to one story, an unconscious Cricket Coogler was supposedly dumped in Apodaca's car at the courthouse, and once he discovered she was dead, he took the body to the desert.
- Apodaca arranged a trip to Albuquerque later on the very same day that Cricket disappeared.

Freddy Barncastle

Attorney Byron Darden's files contain a paper headed "Questions." The name "Fred" also appears on the page, followed by some handwritten questions—either Darden's or someone else's—that seem pointed toward Freddy Barncastle:

On the night of March 30–31, do you remember who were some of
    your late customers?
Do you keep anything for self-protection around the bar or in the
    car?
Have you bought seat covers for your car, from White's Auto, lately?
If so, what did you do with the old ones?
Do you ever loan your car to any of your friends? (Darden Papers)

The idea that Freddy Barncastle might have loaned his gray and blue car is especially interesting. Las Cruces was still a small town. People recognized the cars of others, and drivers sometimes preferred to use someone else's car where recognition of their own was to be avoided. If Barncastle answered W. C. McBride's knock on his tavern door seconds before Cricket was picked up on the street, he could not have been driving his car on that street. W. C. McBride said Freddy personally admitted him to Gateway Gardens in those vital minutes around three in the morning.

- Barncastle's car was a 1941 or 1942 gray Chevrolet with a blue top (colors described as those of the car Cricket Coogler entered). Former border patrolman Sylba Bryant said state police officers Hathaway and Tafoya, as they left town after their second round of investigation, told him they had established the car Cricket entered—a two-tone gray 1941 Chevy—but they could not put a driver in it. Bryant said the policemen told him the suspect car was a coupe. Bryant's was a sedan, leaving Barncastle's as the only such coupe in town.
- Another item listed as "Fact" in the files of attorney Byron Darden indicates that someone, unnamed, claimed to have seen Cricket in El Paso with two men, one named Fred, the other Louie. Barncastle surely knew Cricket Coogler and could have been the Fred seen with her in El Paso.
- A handwritten list in Byron Darden's file titled "Facts" indicates that Cricket Coogler sometimes phoned "Fred" to set up dates, bragging later about having gone out with him. The list included a reference to Gateway Gardens.

- Barncastle was said to be mean when drunk. According to Third Judicial Court records, he was instructed by a judge, following a divorce from his wife, not to attempt to visit his children when drunk.
- After waiting several minutes near the Western Union office, adjacent to the rear of the Gateway Gardens lot, Cricket Coogler knocked on the door of Gateway Gardens after it had closed. No one answered, although McBride had entered only moments ago.
- Freddy Barncastle could have been the local liquor dealer who provided liquor for Dan Sedillo (hand-delivered by state patrolman Salazar) on December 7, 1948, at the party reportedly involving Sedillo, Apodaca, Coogler, and others.
- Dan Sedillo was married to Emelia Barncastle Finch. The name Barncastle is so distinctive in the county that it is generally safe to assume all Barncastles have some familial tie. This could explain Freddy Barncastle's generous hospitality to Emelia's husband Dan whenever he was in town.

Wesley Byrd

- Mechanic Wesley Byrd, tortured in an attempt to coerce his confession, may have lied. His wife and his friends recognized his ability to lie.
- Byrd had flirted with Cricket Coogler in the Tortugas Café and did not hesitate to take risks with women of other ethnic backgrounds, whether in Italy, Texas, or New Mexico.
- Byrd had threatened to kill his wife, according to her employer, Jim Day, and Emma's mother.
- Byrd had caused bruises on his wife Emma, according to her mother. He too, apparently, could be rough with women, especially when drinking.
- Evidence reportedly found in Byrd's home and car included hair similar to Cricket's and lipstick on a shirt of Byrd's. The FBI examined one of Cricket Coogler's shoes, which appeared to be smeared with a blue color similar to the dashboard of Byrd's car. Sid Howard mentioned blue or green paint on the shoe as he initially found it.
- Jim Day told the FBI that Emma had described to him the sight of blood and hair inside Byrd's car on a day not specified but previous to Cricket's disappearance. Emma, however, did not confirm this.

- Byrd left town in July 1949 and had to be summoned back for the 1950 torture trial in Santa Fe.

T. K. Campbell

- Campbell tried to coerce his own secretary into claiming rape by a man named Wayne Clawson, telling her he believed Clawson killed Cricket Coogler, and if only she would cooperate, the Coogler murder could be solved.
- Campbell was described as flustered, stumbling, and perhaps deliberately inept as he questioned those called before the Doña Ana County Grand Jury. For two solid weeks, he focused only on an effort to pinpoint the exact location of Cricket Coogler's body. This appeared to be a stalling tactic, or worse.
- Campbell's position as district attorney enabled a good deal of control over the Coogler case.
- Campbell refused to follow up on the claims by a Canadian woman that Sheriff Apodaca had raped her. Considered by some a womanizer himself, Campbell expressed his opinion that if a woman did not report it immediately, it simply was not rape.
- In 1949 District Attorney Campbell released Jerry Nuzum with wording that sounded overconfident, without details of support for Nuzum's exoneration.

Wayne Clawson

District attorney T. K. Campbell's secretary, Connie Wilder, handled deposits for the DA's office at Mesilla Valley Bank, where she had a few conversations with a teller named Wayne Clawson. She recounted in a personal interview with the author the following: One evening Clawson showed up unannounced at the door of her aunt's house, where she was living at the time. Wayne wanted her to go with him to the popular La Posta restaurant in Old Mesilla for dinner, but Connie had already had dinner and had just washed her hair and put it in curlers. He said he did not want to eat alone, so she found a covering for her wet hair and went with him. He had a couple of drinks with dinner, and Connie began to conclude that perhaps he had been drinking earlier as well.

On the way home, Wayne took a turn onto a deserted dirt road, stopped, and confined her in a stranglehold to attempt a sexual assault. Suddenly headlights approached, and Connie managed to honk the horn. The driver, apparently seeing there was a struggle, made a U-turn, but Clawson sped off. His voice terse with fury, he said to Connie, "Now you're going to get it." Connie managed to get a foot on the accelerator and the car careened toward the big doors of a garage shop apparently closed for the night. Wayne managed to stop the car before it hit the doors, but Connie then got a foot onto the horn and made as much noise as she could. Miraculously, it seemed, a man still inside the garage heard her, came out, and asked what was going on. Connie took the opportunity to escape from the car, and Wayne took off. Connie asked the garage man if he could call a taxi for her. He did.

Although her aunt and her mother discouraged her from calling the police, Connie called them anyway to report the attempted assault. She told her employer, T. K. Campbell, about the incident the following morning. Campbell as DA facilitated her complaint and had Wayne picked up and jailed. Campbell then began a lengthy campaign to convince Connie to file a more serious charge, rape, against Clawson. In one session lasting an hour, he told her he felt that Clawson may have been Cricket Coogler's murderer, a conclusion he said he had come to after several interrogation sessions with Clawson. Campbell told Connie if she would file the right charges, he would be able to link Clawson to the Coogler case and justice could be served. Campbell tried many persuasive means to convince Connie to file rape charges, but she remained unwilling to make a false claim, and her family strongly urged her not to become involved in any way with the Coogler case. Her mother's husband posed the possibility that Tommy Campbell was simply trying to use Connie to get into the headlines and further his political ambitions.

Connie said she was upset by the notion that because of her, Cricket Coogler's murderer might go free, and she talked at length about the situation with Roy Sandman, who was at the time working for Campbell. Sandman listened sympathetically and encouraged her to do what she thought best. Connie determined that she would not change her complaint.

Soon afterward, Connie was walking home when a car pulled up close to her at the corner of Church and Las Cruces. It was Wayne Clawson, freed from jail, who began apologizing and saying he had simply drunk too much that other evening, and he needed to talk to her. He tried to get her to enter the car, assuring her he would never hurt her. Connie would not get into the car, which she remembered only as light-colored. She soon left the office of the district attorney for a better-paying job at White Sands Proving Grounds. Wayne disappeared from Las Cruces; no one seemed to know where he went. (The name "Wayne Clawson" appears in a list contained in the notes of attorney Byron Darden, without any other notation.) In summary:

- Clawson could have been the unnamed "former bank teller" who fingered two men as A&M burglary suspects. He and Cricket may have known similar information about the burglary.
- Clawson left town, and no one seemed to know where he went.
- Clawson could be rough with women, especially after a few drinks.
- Clawson drove a light-colored car.

Joel Coffey

- Taxi driver Joel Coffey was the recipient of a loving phone call from Cricket Coogler around midnight of March 30–31, 1949. Coffey, questioned early in the investigation when Cricket's mother confirmed Cricket had dated him, said he declined Cricket's invitation to meet her that night at the DeLuxe Café and have a drink with her. Nevertheless, he was one of the last persons who spoke to Cricket Coogler, and he probably knew her better than most.

William Love

According to documents in the files of attorney Byron Darden, a twenty-eight-year-old college student, William Love, was picked up and questioned regarding the A&M Business Office safe robbery. An insurance adjuster reported to his company, Fireman's Fund, all he could find out about Love: Love had a prison record in Oregon involving a theft, had welding training while in the navy, went through a second divorce in August 1948, and sported a $2,700, one-and-a-half-carat diamond ring, which he said was left to him by an aunt. Love told Deputy Roy Sandman that his "sister" in California sent him $150 a month and that he received

$75 a month from the government. Love was allegedly the illegitimate son of that California woman. He had worked at one time with steel and welding at a shipyard. He drove a 1947 Oldsmobile convertible (color unknown), which he said his sister gave him. An insurance representative checked on his mother's finances and found that the woman had only a small bank account and a safe-deposit box that had not been used for some time. Love had been employed briefly as a watchman in university housing, but was released when he failed to meet the requirements to be deputized, as was required for the position of watchman. Love was charged with the A&M burglary, released on bond on April 26, 1949 (*EPT*, April 26, 1949), and freed in May, when no substantive connection to the burglary was established.

- Regarding the college burglary, (1) it was speculated that Cricket Coogler was small enough to have climbed through the window entry, and (2) it was said she came home beaten up because she had talked about the burglary. Love and Coogler might have known each other.

Joseph "Little Joe" Montoya

Decades after the case, Doña Ana County Grand Jury member Russell Soper remembered in a videotaped interview: "We considered calling [Lt. Governor] Montoya, but there was no direct evidence that he might have been in the car and we did not call him." If anyone testified that Lt. Governor Montoya was seen in the area March 30–31 or in the mysterious car, the grand jury evidently felt the source or the statement insufficient.

Some of the pieces of the puzzle seem to make more sense if Sheriff Apodaca were protecting an important official such as Montoya—one who had the power to help or hurt him and his family and friends tremendously. If the culprit had been a local fellow or a common soldier, for instance, would there have been enough reason for files to disappear, or for prisoners to be tortured in order to coerce a confession? Would there have been reason for the cold fear that the Doña Ana Grand Jury observed in so many of the people called into the jury room?

- Montoya had flown to El Paso in late February 1949 with Dan Sedillo, and the two paid a visit to Las Cruces. If he followed custom, Sheriff Apodaca would have arranged entertainment on that occasion and perhaps a month later as well, if so requested. Jerry Nuzum, in a video outtake from 1990, stated that three officials from Santa Fe had flown into Las Cruces on the day in question, March 30, 1949. Montoya could have been one of them.

- Montoya's office, according to Tony Hillerman in the video *The Silence of Cricket Coogler*, checked out a state car for a period including March 31, 1949, but this researcher could find no documentation in the state archives to confirm this. The make and color of that car would, of course, have been a most interesting detail. Another story from the video is that the state car in question burned near Roswell in a timely and convenient fashion.

- Montoya was named by an FBI informant as the recipient of gambling protection money.

- An off-camera voice in an outtake from the same video expresses agreement with Jack Flynn that Montoya had a "rough" appetite with women.

- Even though Montoya had the most to lose, politically, if he were tied to the Coogler case, his name seemed untouchable. Yet, according to a 1980 presentation to NMSU by journalist Bill Diven, the Coogler case hung around Montoya's neck "like an albatross."

- From his home in Santa Fe, it was a short drive for Montoya if he needed to attend a meeting in Albuquerque in the early evening hours of March 31, 1949.

Luther Mosley

- Truck driver Luther "Mr. Green Eyes" Mosley appeared to argue with Cricket at some early point on March 30, 1949. They were also seen together twice in the DeLuxe Café that morning, perhaps during Cricket's working hours.

- Mosley maintained a keen interest in Cricket Coogler for at least four hours on the evening she disappeared.

- Mosley followed Cricket on foot as she left the DeLuxe Café for the last time.

- Oddly, Jerry Nuzum said nothing at all about the encounter with

Mosley outside the DeLuxe, describing only his exchange with manager Bob Ash. (Bob Ash, however, did recall the Nuzum/Mosley encounter.)

- Mosley said he "got to thinking" as he observed the car following Cricket along Church Street. Something or someone deterred his former apparent determination to be with Cricket Coogler.

Jerry Nuzum

- On the night in question, Pittsburgh Steeler Jerry Nuzum left his wife and children home, packing for a move, while he "made the rounds" until almost three in the morning, appearing in several bars both alone and in the occasional company of Cricket Coogler.
- Nuzum was observed flirting mildly with Cricket, playing shuffleboard with her, then struggling to put her in his car, twice, in the early morning hours of March 31, 1949. His purpose in putting her in the car could have been to deliver her somewhere.
- Nuzum's car reportedly had a dent in the underside, as well as substances that no one except Dr. Rife would define as human blood/tissue.
- Nuzum left the DeLuxe Café alone about 3:00, just as Cricket Coogler was last seen alive, and reports vary about whether he walked to the bar next door or drove away. If he did not go home, he could have reinvolved himself with Cricket Coogler a few minutes later, in his car or a borrowed one.
- Nuzum's landlady withdrew her support of his alibi, that is, that he was home by 2:55 a.m. Two witnesses said Nuzum was embracing Cricket in front the café just after 3:00 a.m.
- Nuzum abruptly checked out of New Mexico A&M and left town March 31, 1949, the afternoon following Cricket's disappearance.
- Nuzum and Lamar Bailey were in El Paso the evening of March 27, the same evening Cricket and her friend Josie were in El Paso. Nuzum could conceivably have been the unnamed husky man who saw Cricket and Josie to the bus stop that evening.
- Nuzum was a friend of Happy Apodaca, as well as Robert Templeton (described later in this chapter).
- Nuzum was in Albuquerque by the early evening hours of March 31, 1949, the day of Cricket's disappearance.

Jerry Nuzum's guilt or innocence was not established in his 1951 trial. The evidence just was not there, according to the judge's directed verdict.

Some positive facts did work in favor of Nuzum's innocence. He volunteered, twice, to come to Las Cruces; paid for the trips with his own money; and invariably, as seen on video five decades later, sounds like a good guy—a little brash, sometimes sheepish, but straightforward in his telling of events. Nuzum voluntarily stayed in jail, seeming confident that the matter would be cleared up as soon as the police talked to a few more witnesses. No shred of evidence was found inside Nuzum's car, which was systematically dismantled.

Carlos Salas

- State policeman Carlos Salas, stationed in Las Cruces, was named by FBI informants as a recipient of gambling protection money, and as one included in a mysterious jewelry-store meeting with Robert Milkman of Valley Country Club and other key players.
- Jerry Nuzum once remarked that Carlos Salas considered himself "Dick Tracy" (*EPHP*, May 11, 1949). Salas, somewhat an enigma, was described alternately by townspeople as arrogant and humane, condescending and courageous.
- Salas's log book shows he was home by 11:00 p.m. on March 30, 1949, but it is assumed Salas kept his own log book.
- Salas could have driven a black state police car, like the one Mary Foy described, into which she said two policemen dumped Cricket Coogler.
- Salas was present during the torture of Wesley Byrd, but said he felt sick and wandered far enough away that he could not see what was going on.
- As he testified at the torture trial, Salas seemed to press as lightly as possible on his friend Apodaca, consistently pointing only to Beasley as the one he observed placing a padlock on Wesley Byrd.
- Salas was a close family friend of Happy Apodaca and was often in his company.
- Reporter Alice Gruver mentioned that Salas laughed at her questions about the A&M robbery.

I. E. "Sally" Salazar

- State policeman Salazar was stationed in Las Cruces on March 30, 1949.
- Salazar said he did not know where he was that night, since his records had been seized.
- Salazar could have driven a black state police car, like the one Mary Foy described.
- Salazar was a husky man, like the policeman described by Mary Foy (although Foy, when shown Salazar in the courtroom, confounded this idea by saying he was not the man she saw).
- Lauren Welch, given a choice between Salazar and Salas as the state policeman who beat him to coerce a confession to the murder of Cricket Coogler, said it was the "big one." Salazar was the larger of the two.
- Salazar consistently backed Sheriff Apodaca in denying that any torture of Wesley Byrd occurred at the desert gravesite of Cricket Coogler. Salazar said that when he got to the scene the second time, those present were getting into Apodaca's car to leave. Byrd remembers it differently, saying that Salazar returned to the site about the same time as Apodaca, Sandman, and the second bicycle lock.
- After the trip to the desert, Salazar told FBI agent McConnell that Byrd "got out of the sheriff's car and walked with ease" back into the courthouse. "Ease" seems an unlikely descriptor, considering what Byrd had endured. This casts doubt on Salazar's other statements.

Victor Salazar

- "Second-floor governor" Victor Salazar, the handsome and powerful head of the 1949 Bureau of Revenue, was purported to have political savvy and power second to none in the state except maybe Senator Dennis Chavez. As virtual governor, Salazar had oversight of agencies for law enforcement and the power to give personal directives.
- V. Salazar held many responsibilities in handling money for the state of New Mexico. Privately, his insurance agency was the number-one source for the state of New Mexico's insurance. "Follow the money" theories included Victor Salazar.
- V. Salazar was the treasurer for the State Democratic Party organization

and was therefore the logical recipient for any gambling payoffs intended for the party.
- V. Salazar could have made a short drive to Albuquerque in the early evening hours of March 31, 1949.

Dan Sedillo

- Several weeks before her disappearance, Cricket was said to be in a hotel room with New Mexico corporation commissioner Dan Sedillo, fully clothed, having passed out from drinking alcohol. At another time prior to her disappearance, Cricket was allegedly tied to a table in a motel and assaulted.
- A service-station employee apparently named Sedillo as the man whose car he serviced in Las Cruces on the morning of March 31, 1949. The station employee said the man had been drinking. Sedillo's records were scoured for service-station receipts, but none were located.
- Sedillo refused grand jury questioning, instead reading a brief statement in which he simply denied ever being with Cricket Coogler— seemingly nullified by his own later statements about his being "singled out" from among many men who had been with Cricket Coogler.
- Sedillo had lived in Las Cruces and knew the area.
- Sedillo's proof that he had been in Santa Fe at the time of Coogler's death was weak: a few typed documents with that date.
- Regardless of his denials, Sedillo was seen by more than one person in Las Cruces the night of March 30 and/or morning of March 31, 1949. A reliable source, attorney LaFel Oman, said Cricket was partying with some state officials that evening, and Sedillo could have been one of them. Jerry Nuzum stated that three officials from Santa Fe had flown into Las Cruces on the day in question—March 30, 1949.
- Sedillo had access to cars with official state license plates.
- Sedillo could have been available for a meeting in Albuquerque in the early evening hours of March 31, 1949.

Robert Templeton

On July 5, 1949, Robert Templeton, described at first only as a twenty-five-year-old farmer, was arrested at his home, which was about a mile from the desert grave where Cricket Coogler's body was found. The Doña Ana County Grand Jury had indicted him for a June 6, 1949, assault with intent to rape a woman who worked as a grocery clerk/waitress. Carl Glick, who lived nearby and responded to the woman's request for help, drove her back to Las Cruces (*EPHP*, July 5, 1949).

The alleged rape victim apparently could not be located for service of a subpoena, because a bench warrant was issued for her on January 23, 1950. Nothing further happened on the case until August 23, 1951, when it was dismissed, according to Third Judicial Court archives. Templeton appeared in July 1949 headlines as a new suspect in the Coogler case, but the questioning must have cleared him satisfactorily, and Templeton's name disappeared from the newspapers.

Robert Templeton was listed in the back pages of the 1948 Las Cruces telephone directory under "Rural Route 1," with no spouse's name in the customary parentheses used throughout the directory.

- The Third Judicial Court archives contain a witness subpoena for Templeton in which Sheriff Martinez was directed to "bring the pin found on the dress on the body of Ovida Coogler," apparently thought to be in Robert Templeton's possession. No other mention of this pin was found.
- The *El Paso Herald-Post* reported that a private investigator saw spots of blood on the inside roof of Templeton's car, and that when Templeton was arrested, he said he had a gun.
- Templeton knew the area where Cricket's body was left very well, as he lived only about a mile away.
- Templeton owned a 1941 cream-colored Chevrolet.
- Templeton, reportedly a bartender and friend of Jerry Nuzum, was divorced from his wife on the interesting date of March 31, 1949.
- According to the *El Paso Herald-Post*, Templeton entered a Las Cruces store on Saturday, July 2, 1949, and told his ex-wife, "I am going to kill you at three o'clock tomorrow." He did not.

Unnamed Soldier from the Green Frog Café

A soldier, or a man posing as a soldier, was in Las Cruces on the evening of March 30–31, 1949, having met Corinne Massingale for a date.

She said he boarded a bus back to El Paso about 1:30 on the morning of March 31.

- The soldier established some relationship with Cricket Coogler, even if for only one evening, at El Paso's Green Frog Café, three days before she disappeared.
- His nickname was reportedly written on a photo stub found in the billfold of Cricket Coogler, but this nickname was never made public. Jerry Nuzum's nickname was "Bruiser."
- Although neither Fort Bliss nor White Sands military contained any record of the name the soldier had given Cricket and Corinne, whoever this fellow was, he was in the right place at the right time.

Lauren Welch

The "Kansas suspect," Lauren (sometimes spelled Loren) Welch, a former Las Cruces bus driver, told FBI special agent Finis Sims that he had been "keeping company" with Cricket Coogler until late January 1949.

Welch told FBI agent McConnell that sometime in December 1948, about four o'clock in the morning, Cricket got out of a 1937 Lincoln Zephyr coupe belonging to someone named "Jack" in front of the Coogler home, then got into Welch's car. (Welch confirmed he had been waiting for her at that unlikely hour.) Welch said he and Cricket, whom he described as "pretty well drunk" at the time, just rode around for a while, but then Cricket hit him and he hit her back and then took her home. Welch said Cricket had once made an attempt to jump out of his car. He did not elaborate on why Cricket hit him or attempted to jump out of his car at some time. He described her as "oversexed when drinking." He said he had given Cricket his military dog tags and wanted them back.

- Welch owned a 1939 four-door cream-colored Oldsmobile, which he said had been repossessed two weeks prior to March 31, 1949.
- Welch said he saw Cricket Coogler in her waitress uniform on a downtown block after six o'clock the evening of March 30, 1949. He could have talked with her at that time as well.
- Lauren Welch knew Cricket Coogler well enough to offer her his military dog tags, well enough for her to confide a great deal in him.

- Welch admitted to hitting Coogler on one occasion, and she had once attempted to jump out of his car.
- Welch left Las Cruces on a Kansas-bound bus April 1, 1949, not long after midnight. He and his wife apparently separated at that point.

Cricket Coogler entered a car on March 31, 1949, but that car was rarely described twice as the same color, make, or model. For a summary of the various cars nominated for consideration, see appendix II, "The Many Colored Cars."

14   What Happened to People after the Case

Happy Apodaca

Happy Apodaca walked out of La Tuna prison at the stroke of midnight April 13, 1952, ducked into a friend's car, and lay down in the back seat. All three prisoners, Apodaca, Beasley, and Sandman, had received time off for good behavior (*LCSN*, April 14, 1952).

According to Chope Benavides, Happy Apodaca became a successful bill collector, once obtaining payment for a business bill Chope had been unable to collect. "He did collect it for me," Chope said on videotape. "He probably threatened them—in a nice way. . . . He did not charge me. Others he did charge" (VI). One should hope Apodaca would not charge Chope Benavides, who had often interceded to minimize problems for Sheriff Apodaca.

Benavides described efforts to tone down Apodaca's actions for his own good, telling him, for example, that such activities as intense arm wrestling were not appropriate for a sheriff. Chope worried that someone would make Happy Apodaca mad, and there would be serious trouble. He sought help from Santa Fe. Chope said, "I called [comptroller J. D.] Hannah, a good friend of mine. [Another] friend, Mr. Rodriguez, a politician from San Miguel, and I drove Happy up there [to Santa Fe]. . . . Hannah gave Happy good advice, and Happy promised, but he never did settle down" (VI).

Just prior to the 1948 election, at a political rally at Howell's Bar in La Mesa, Sheriff Apodaca had arbitrarily demanded cash from the bartender, and when she refused unless he gave her a check, Chope Benavides, sitting only two barstools away at the time, simply handed Apodaca a twenty-dollar bill. Apodaca gave the bartender a withering glare and returned to whatever he had been doing (AI).

In another debt-collection effort, Happy Apodaca removed the motor from a water well and told the owners that when the debt was paid, he would return the motor. Without house water, the debtors likely found a way to pay the outstanding bill (AI).

In 1957, Happy Apodaca sent the following undated, handwritten letter to the attorney general of the United States, marked received December 17:

Dear Sir: Will you please give me an opinion if a person indicted and convicted of the following violations, civil rights and conspiracy, will be able to run and hold a public office? I would also like to learn if such violations are felonies or misdemeanors. Thanking you in advance, I remain, Very truly yours, A. L. Apodaca (NARA)

The current U.S. pardon attorney's office says his petition was denied. However, his crimes were not felonies, and therefore pardons were unnecessary. The reply to Apodaca's letter probably confirmed for him the Class A misdemeanor category of his crime. A penalty of one year or less (the sentences of Apodaca, Beasley, and Sandman) placed their offenses in the category of Class A misdemeanors. The General Federal Conspiracy statute carried a five-year penalty (Class D felony), except where the crime conspired to required a lesser maximum sentence. Violation of civil rights was a misdemeanor with a one year or $1,000 fine, or both. That being the maximum for the actual violation, it would also have been the maximum for the conspiracy count (*Apodaca v. US 188 F2d. 932* [1951]).

Apodaca did indeed run for office again. After serving as justice of the peace in the town of Mesilla for ten years, he won the 1974 election as magistrate judge. Wording from Happy Apodaca's campaign ad in the *Sun-News* of November 13, 1974: "I stand for justice, every one [*sic*] will be innocent until proven guilty. . . . I think that my eight years of experience as justice of the peace in Mesilla and eight years with the New Mexico State Police have given me plenty of understanding of the law required for a person on the bench."

His election as magistrate judge did not come easily, even though the count showed he had won by 1,384 votes. More than fifty complaints were registered concerning voting procedures (disappearance of pencils, for example, which would eliminate write-in votes for Apodaca's opponent in the race, Dan Lowry). One anonymous letter to the editor chastised Lowry for an advertisement that read, "Happy Apodaca Convicted—Is This the Type of Person You Want as Your Magistrate Judge?" (*LCSN*, November 11, 1974).

In April 1978, Apodaca was removed from his magistrate position for judicial misconduct, after he failed to disqualify himself in a case involving his son (Pat Henry, *EPT*, October 31, 1982). But this did not disqualify him from running again, and he was again a candidate for the same office in the June 1978 primary. In a paid advertisement in the *Sun-News* on May 19, 1978, Apodaca accused a member of the magistrate's staff of filing the complaint that resulted in his removal from the magistrate position. A magistrate court clerk, Annie N., immediately retaliated by filing a slander suit against Apodaca, the outcome of which was not reported. In 1978 voters were asked to "Support Poor Happy" (*LCSN*, May 19, 1978), but he was defeated by Benjamin Rios. Apodaca's only apparent stronghold was found in the South Valley, where he won two Mesilla precincts and Sunland Park (formerly Anapra).

People who have been the recipients of favors important to their families do not forget. Some probably felt Apodaca had paid his debt to society. And he continued his outgoing, smiling, and confident ways, unbowed, even in temporary humble occupations such as vending-machine stocker (AI).

Some years after the Coogler case faded, Apodaca had a brush with death in a high-speed accident in which his car hit a sixteen-wheeler's engine, fusing his car to the truck. Dr. Dan Maddox remembered that it was hard to believe Apodaca survived, but "the top of his car opened the heavens to him, and he flew out, forty to sixty feet in the air, landing on his hands and breaking an arm, which I treated" (VI). Apodaca's right arm was thereafter a bit shorter than the other one and permanently crooked, exactly right to deliver a boxer's jab.

One story circulated from Apodaca's magistrate days was that a man described as a hippie came into Apodaca's little courtroom and announced that he was disqualifying the judge. Apodaca came out from his bench, beat the man to the floor, then calmly returned to his bench and opened the session (AI).

In 1979, only one year after he was removed from his magistrate position, sixty-seven-year-old Apodaca, still collecting debts for others, appeared at the Vado home of an elderly woman and announced that he was there to see one of her family about a bad check. When he learned that person was not there, he said he was seizing a chain saw and holding it until the check cleared. When the woman tried to prevent that, Apodaca shoved her against a car. She called the police, and when they caught up with Apodaca on the way back to Las Cruces, he had two new charges against him: driving under the influence and reckless driving, reportedly because Apodaca would not pull over and refused to get out of his car when a deputy stopped him. Apodaca was released on $150 bond (*LCSN*, February 12, 1979).

But Happy Apodaca was right about his unshakable popularity. For example, he was elected in February 1954 as president of the Holy Cross Booster Club, which helped raise funds for Holy Cross School.

In 1981, Happy Apodaca died at age sixty-nine of an apparent heart attack, falling from the roof of his home. About six hundred people attended his funeral. Cars in the funeral procession formed an almost unbroken line from the San Albino Church on Mesilla's town plaza, where his funeral Mass was held, to the Masonic Cemetery in Las Cruces—about two miles. His larger-than-life, checkered history had earned this status. Parking overflowed on the adjacent streets of Compress and Brown Road. Some of the mourners must have stood very near Cricket Coogler's final gravesite, because in that Masonic Cemetery, only thirty paces—across a narrow path—separate Happy Apodaca's grave from hers.

Lamar Bailey

The convict who slept on the Nuzums' sofa at least once was indicted in August 1949 for conspiracy to prevent the postmaster at Radium Springs, just north of Las Cruces, from performing his duties. Apparently Bailey physically threw the postmaster from his office, which was located in a corner of the hotel managed by the postmaster (*LCSN*, August 22, 1949). In August 1949, Bailey failed to appear when summoned before the federal grand jury in Santa Fe. He was indicted in connection with the purchase of five jewelry stores with fraudulent checks totaling $10,000. In September, Bailey was the subject of a statewide search, wanted for assault and battery, carrying a concealed weapon, and disturbing the peace. Bailey was also wanted in El Paso, Texas, for multiple offenses. By October 2, 1949, a Las Cruces headline announced that Bailey was the most-wanted man in New Mexico; but soon the search was called off, and Bailey escaped from the front pages and from justice, at least for a few years. In 1956 he was found guilty of assault and battery; he appealed, and because the state read testimony instead of producing a key witness in person, the verdict was reversed (www.fastcase.com).

Freddy Barncastle

Freddy Barncastle lived only three years after Cricket Coogler's death. It was said that his hair had suddenly turned white, perhaps from a medical condition. He died in 1952 at age thirty-nine, and his military funeral service at St. Genevieve's Church was attended by one of the largest crowds ever to attend services in Las Cruces. He had been hospitalized for three days (with an apparent blood disorder) and received numerous transfusions of what must have been an unusual blood type, because some donors from nearby White Sands Proving Grounds were recruited in futile efforts to save his life.

Hubert Beasley

In a letter to Governor Mabry, released September 24, 1950, in the *Santa Fe New Mexican*, State Chief of Police Beasley still protested his innocence of the torture charges. Beasley nevertheless asked to be relieved of his position, and Governor Mabry obliged. After serving his prison term, Beasley returned to Tucumcari, where he was appointed police chief—not an elected office. The New Mexico Sheriffs and Police Association elected a new president, Hubert Beasley's successor in that position, and prompted this editorial response:

> Election of Albuquerque Police Chief Paul Shaver as president of the New Mexico Sheriffs and Police association should give that organization a seriously needed lift toward public respect.
> Shaver is a clean officer and a good one who came up through the ranks of the Albuquerque police department. He respects the law.
> The association he heads has had an unfortunate record of rowdyism and disrespect for the law. The members and the public should welcome leadership of Shaver's type. (*SFNM*, October 26, 1950)

Eventually Beasley retired to his ranch, and died in 1971.

Wesley Byrd

"Wesley Byrd contemplated suing for damages, but then returned suddenly and alone to Altapass, North Carolina and went back to cutting timber. On January 24, 1967, a half-brother shot him during an argument and he bled to death" (Bill Diven, *AJ*, February 23, 1986).

T. K. Campbell

In 1950 district attorney T. K. Campbell returned to the practice of law in Las Cruces, moving his law offices into renovated spaces from time to time. He partnered in a very successful and lucrative real estate development effort in the North Valley and other neighborhoods. He took over settlement of some prominent estates, one of which included an elegant old house and property on University Avenue in Las Cruces and a ranch near Kingston, New Mexico. Campbell retired from the New Mexico Bar Association in 1995 after fifty years of membership. He died August 3, 1997, at the age of eighty-one.

Dennis Chavez

U.S. Senator Dennis Chavez continued as senator until his death in 1962. He periodically broke with his party, as he had in subtly supporting a Republican for governor in 1950. Controversy surrounded him. In the 1952 election, his challenger, Major General Patrick Hurley, charged that "over 100 election districts had unscreened booths, over 20,000 ballots were marked by pencil (a violation of state law) and showed signs of erasures" (*Newsweek*, May 11, 1953).

Aided by an FBI investigator, the Senate Campaign Committee discovered that 19,000 ballots had been burned on the order of district judge William T. Scoggin Jr., who explained that the ballot boxes had been needed for local elections (*Newsweek*, May 11, 1953). So many irregularities were uncovered that a U.S. Senate committee pronounced it "impossible to distinguish the free and honest vote," and declared that no one had been elected in the race between Hurley and Chavez (*Time*, March 22, 1954). The decision went to a Senate floor vote, and Chavez retained the seat.

Chavez went on to become a much-admired figure and held important status as the first native-born Hispanic to serve in the U.S. Senate. He maintained a reputation for courageous objection to Senator Joe McCarthy's communist-hunting hearings, and as an advocate for human and civil rights. New Mexico owes Senator Chavez thanks for his efforts to establish its White Sands Missile Range, Sandia Laboratory, Holloman Air Force Base, and other installations critical to the state's economy to this day. His archived papers reveal his concern with the problems of individual constituents, and his personal involvement in service to them. But by the mid-1950s, according to author Robert Caro's *Master of the Senate*, Senator Chavez had a severe problem with alcohol, sometimes evident on the Senate floor.

Among 142 honorary pallbearers at the funeral of Dennis Chavez on November 21, 1962, were Joseph M. Montoya, Victor Salazar, Dan Sedillo, Filo Sedillo, Judge Charles R. Brice, Justice James McGhee, and Governor Edwin Mechem.

Ollie Coogler

Ollie Coogler remained in Las Cruces, expertly altering clothing for the better department stores such as the White House (formerly Dunlap's White House). A co-worker described her as stately, quiet, pleasant—a person with whom it was a pleasure to work (AI). Ollie was a member of the Fifth Street Baptist Church. She remarried in 1953 to A. C. Taylor, who died twenty years later in 1973. Ollie died at her home in 1994 at the age of eighty-seven. At a Las Cruces showing of *The Silence of Cricket Coogler*, a relative of Ollie's approached the host and told him that during Ollie's funeral, someone entered her home and stole as many papers and materials having to do with the case that could be found in a rushed burglary. The burglar was never identified (AI).

Thomas J. Mabry

After his term as governor ended, Tom Mabry reentered law practice with his two sons. He acknowledged criticism of his tenure as governor, particularly about retaining state police chief Hubert Beasley after Beasley was indicted and convicted of torture, and about not firing Victor Salazar, who was "unpopular with many of the statehouse crowd" (*LCSN*, December 28, 1950). After completion of his term as governor, Mabry retired from politics. He died in Albuquerque on December 23, 1962.

Edwin L. Mechem

Governor Mechem began his term with major proposals, including these pledges, listed in the December 30, 1950, *New York Times*:

1. To put the state police on a merit system under an effective nonpartisan police commission, in place of a freehand appointive system
2. To supplant one-man liquor control [Tom Montoya] with a state board
3. To put state court judgeships on a nonpolitical basis
4. To consolidate the Public Service Commission [W. W. Nichols, chair], frequently charged with prejudicial administration, with the State Corporation Commission [Dan Sedillo's office], and overhaul the latter
5. To free the State Highway Commission [Burton Dwyre and Rufus Sedillo] from political control

Mechem also vowed to eliminate fifteen "deadheads," whose compensation totaled $50,000 a year. He identified two of these "deadheads" as state treasurer H. R. Rodgers and attorney Filo Sedillo (one of Dan Sedillo's defense attorneys), who was at that time consumers' counsel for the Public Service Commission (*AJ*, October 15, 1950).

Mechem remained governor until 1955, was elected again in 1957, and yet again in 1961. After U.S. Senator Dennis Chavez died in November 1962, Edwin L. Mechem resigned the governorship so that his lieutenant governor, Tom Bolack, could (in a one-month interim governorship) appoint Mechem as Chavez's temporary replacement. Such a short window of time existed because Jack Campbell had already won the 1962 election and would take the governor's office—and the right to appoint an interim senator—on January 1, 1963. Mechem intended to keep the senatorial seat through the next election (1964), but Joseph "Little Joe" Montoya, then a U.S. representative, became a candidate, defeated Mechem, and took Dennis Chavez's Senate seat back for the Democrats. In 1964, Ed Mechem returned to the practice of law. He died in Albuquerque on November 27, 2002.

Joseph "Little Joe" Montoya

Joseph Montoya was lieutenant governor for 1949–1950 and again for 1955–1957. In January 1957, Montoya resigned from the post because he was appointed as temporary U.S. representative to the seat of Antonio Manuel Fernandez—who had suffered a severe stroke, was in a coma, and never learned he had been reelected. Fernandez's death was announced one day after the election (*AJ*, November 7, 1956). Because Fernandez was a Democrat, the Democrats were able to name a temporary replacement until a special election in April. Montoya was so named and subsequently won the April election. He kept his House of Representatives seat until 1964, when he defeated Ed Mechem for Chavez's U.S. Senate seat.

James Matray's online biography describes Senator Montoya as an early critic of U.S. military action in Vietnam. Senator Montoya was a member of the Watergate panel, where he was criticized in the media for methodically reading questions from cards, regardless of whether those questions had just been addressed or were relevant. Matray: "Columnist Art Buchwald advised that when Montoya began questioning, it was a good time for television viewers to visit the bathroom. . . . His defenders, however, blamed the negative image on inadequate staff work and the disadvantage of being the last questioner."

Montoya suffered a good deal of unwelcome publicity having to do with newspaper reports that (1) the Internal Revenue Service had refused to audit his tax returns for twenty years, despite a history of late filings; (2) he had created seven dummy committees to launder $100,000 in campaign contributions; (3) he had exploited his position to lease his property for post offices and other federal buildings; and (4) he accepted a campaign contribution from Tongsun Park ("Koreagate" figure who gave large cash donations and sumptuous parties for selected members of the U.S. Congress), allegedly to oppose economic sanctions against South Korea's regime. However, no legal action was taken against Montoya (Matray).

Although Montoya's early career was more often linked with Senator Clinton Anderson's network than that of Senator Dennis Chavez, Montoya was obviously a student and a beneficiary of Chavez's power. And the two certainly knew each other for years—perhaps even as early as 1934–1938, when Montoya worked in the U.S. Department of the Interior while a law student in Washington. On September 6, 1935, Senator Chavez's secretary filed the following note. Whether the note was dictated by the senator or was the secretary's own words is unclear:

Joe Montoya called me right after his conference with the detective and started to tell me in Spanish over the phone what had happened and I asked him to refrain. They called him in for a second conference and asked him why he had called me and why I had asked him to refrain from talking. It seems that the wires are tapped for it is a mystery to me how they can detect a phone call into this office. I am not saying anything over the phone. In fact I am not saying anything. I am keeping my mouth shut. (Dennis Chavez Papers)

Assuming the Joe Montoya mentioned is indeed Joseph M. Montoya, the note allows only a dim but provocative glimpse into the matter, since the subject the detective wanted to talk about is not revealed.

In the 1976 election, Montoya lost his Senate seat to astronaut Harrison Schmitt. In that campaign, Cleo Montoya, the widow of Montoya's brother, headed the Democrats for Schmitt Committee. Montoya died two years later, in 1978.

Jerry Nuzum

Jerry Nuzum played five seasons for the Pittsburgh Steelers after his directed verdict of not guilty. Ten years passed before he returned to New Mexico. He told reporter Pat Henry that "it [the charge of murder] put me in a bind for twenty years . . . twenty thousand dollars in expenses—a fortune in the 1950s. And it was so embarrassing to be accused of a crime like that. You can't ever live it down . . ." (*EPT*, October 31, 1982). It took him years to repay everyone he owed, including the money Steelers owner Art Rooney had advanced him against his own salary. Nuzum said his application to the prestigious Pittsburgh Athletic Association was in jeopardy when a board member questioned him about what happened in New Mexico in 1949; but Nuzum was ultimately accepted as a member (VI).

On videotape, Nuzum also gave his opinion that (1) the person responsible for Cricket's death was one of three men from Santa Fe who had flown into Las Cruces for a party planned for the night of March 30, 1949; and (2) Apodaca, Beasley, and Sandman were "thrown to the wolves to cover for the higher-ups." He also said that "guilt reached all the way to Washington, D.C." (VI).

At the time of his death, April 23, 1997, Nuzum was a grandfather and CEO of a successful Chevrolet dealership in Uniontown, Pennsylvania.

Carlos Salas

On September 28, 1951, the *Sun-News* reported a mysterious telegram sent to state policeman Carlos Salas which read, "Join me next month." It was signed "Cricket Coogler." Whether the message was a threat or a prank was not determined. Carlos Salas was moved to Carrizozo, New Mexico, lost his rank through "reorganization," retired after twenty-six years of service, ran a bar in Albuquerque for a time, then returned to Doña Ana County, where he died at the age of seventy-five in September 1981.

Victor Salazar

On May 13, 1950, Victor Salazar told the *Albuquerque Journal* that he dropped out of the race for lieutenant governor one week after he entered it because of the pressure of personal business, although he had resigned his post as head of the Bureau of Revenue to make the race. He said he was confident he would have won if he had stayed in the race, even though some of his friends believed he had made a mistake in filing for such a minor office. Although he sat on a speaker's platform the evening before the kickoff of the 1950 state convention of the Democratic Party, which nominated John Miles for governor, Salazar did not attend the rest of the convention. At that convention, Salazar was replaced as treasurer of the state Democratic Party by J. Wade Miles—son of John Miles, the gubernatorial candidate upset by Mechem.

It is no surprise that Salazar's insurance agency, the Victor Agency in Albuquerque, had been the number-one agency for the state's business in 1948–1949 (*SFNM*, July 11, 1949). Salazar purchased a Gulf service station in Albuquerque in April 1950, as well as an adjoining property on which he planned a multistoried office building (*AJ*, April 20, 1950). He returned to a quieter business life. Victor Salazar died in 1985.

Roy Sandman

Roy Sandman said he intended to solve the Coogler case when he was freed from La Tuna Federal Prison. On April 18, 1953, less than a year after his release, Roy Sandman was found dead of an apparent suicide in the Las Cruces warehouse of Border Truckline, for which Sandman worked at the time. The FBI said an embezzlement charge had been made against Sandman, which might offer a reason for a suicide, but his death certificate lists the cause of death as "undetermined." The coroner's jury reported his death was from a gunshot wound, the cause of which was not known.

Sandman's stepdaughter, Sharon Thurber Johnson of Albuquerque, said Roy had been shot in the back of the head and that no autopsy was performed.

On the night of his death, Roy dropped me off at the First Baptist Church for my youth group. I was to get a ride back home with friends. While on the way, Roy was pulled over by several men in a car, claiming to be from the FBI. They told him that they would meet him at the warehouse, where he was the manager. . . . My stepfather was a moral man and had been a criminal investigator in the Army for 20 years. He had three Bronze Stars and an EAME [European-African-Middle Eastern Campaign] ribbon and was in two different concentration camps. Not the sort to commit suicide. . . . (VI)

[Author's note: What appear to be autopsy photos in the collection of Sheriff Jim Flanagan, MS 259 in New Mexico State University's Rio Grande Historical Collection, show Sandman's body with a gunshot on the side of the head, just above the ear.]

William T. Scoggin Jr.

W. T. (Bill) Scoggin Jr. remained a district judge of the Third Judicial District, covering Doña Ana, Lincoln, and Otero counties, until his death in December 1966.

Dan Sedillo

On March 10, 1952, corporation commissioner Dan Sedillo was asked to answer charges of exceeding the commission's budget, failure to pay bills on a current basis, discrepancies on per diem vouchers, payments made from the wrong funds, wrongful collection of fees from public utilities, and paying too much for an inventory study. Apparently, accounting for employee hours was quite lax as well. The commissioners assured auditors that procedures had already been tightened up, and that payroll reductions and reassignments should solve the problems (*LCSN*, March 10, 1952).

Dan Sedillo retired from the state of New Mexico after thirty-four years of service, including eight years as state corporation commissioner, as a port of entry official, as an employee in the Liquor and Gasoline Tax divisions, and as field auditor for the Welfare Department. He died September 4, 1979, in a veterans' hospital in Albuquerque. He was seventy-six.

Rufus Sedillo

Rufus Sedillo, assistant state highway engineer, was said to have partied with Cricket Coogler, Happy Apodaca, Aurelia McFarland, and Dan Sedillo. Yet Rufus was questioned minimally. Rufus's "dozing statehouse spot," as the *Santa Fe New Mexican* (November 5, 1950) characterized his job as assistant state highway engineer, paid a salary of $8,400. His position continued through Governor Mabry's tenure. One of Governor Mechem's first actions was to free the State Highway Engineer's Office of political influence, and presumably free it of its top two administrators, which would have included Rufus Sedillo.

Epilogue

In the Coogler case, investigators, bona fide or not, had to follow sticky threads in several directions, as if navigating a spiderweb. From the center of the case, marked by the body of Cricket Coogler, they struggled toward answers they hoped were waiting all along the edges of the web. Many of those answers, although valuable, had nothing to do with who killed Cricket Coogler.

The absence of records created huge gaps for those trying to navigate the web. Many documents about the case were misplaced immediately. Others were lost during moves to new locations. The county courthouse, sheriff's office, and judicial buildings all moved to new and improved locations over the next several years. A number of officials, including judges, magistrates, officers of the law, the district attorneys, and/or their staff members, had access to those records. A county sheriff in the 1990s said that as soon as he took office, he looked for files on the Cricket Coogler case. He found absolutely none.

A legal researcher reported that she could not locate the original district court case against Apodaca, and for some reason the Apodaca case is not listed in Shepard's (a nationally recognized citations service) or in the *Federal Supplement.* Some records were simply destroyed routinely and legitimately, according to New Mexico's record-retention guidelines. According to staff in the Third Judicial District, for example, trial transcripts are not kept more than twenty years and may be destroyed after the death of a defendant.

Current microfilm records about the case in the Third Judicial District offer only bare-bones logs, legal motions, and subpoena copies.

Some trails of investigation were effectively blocked by witnesses who refused to answer questions, or by what appeared to be gross negligence on the part of those who should have been the ones most dedicated to solving the Coogler case. Governor Tom Mabry and "second-floor governor" Victor Salazar surely wanted no threads to lead into the chambers of state government. They sent their state police chief to personally oversee the handling, perhaps the direction, of the case. And in Washington, DC, Senators Dennis Chavez and Clinton Anderson would have wanted to avoid the embarrassment of a high-placed state official or anyone in their extended circles of political party, family, and friends.

In 1949–1950, many people seemed to feel fairly sure they had figured out who killed Cricket Coogler. Arguments and theories continue even today across café counters and kitchen tables, although some who lived in the area in 1949 seem less convinced now of their early skills in logic, or rightfully distrust their fifty-year-old memories.

In the year 2004, after a presentation of the video *The Silence of Cricket Coogler* in Las Cruces, Doña Ana County Grand Jury member R. A. Durio was asked, "Who do you think was in that car with Cricket Coogler?" He said, "It was one of those politicians, but I don't know which one." His wife Mary added: "Every one of those politicians was involved."

Videotaped for the same film, the unforgettable Chope Benavides, standing behind his famous bar in La Mesa, gave this succinct opinion: "I don't think Happy killed the girl. But some of his friends did."

The only certainty was that Cricket Coogler died, intentionally or accidentally, whether by blunt instrument, alcohol poisoning, being run over by an automobile, or some other cause. Regardless of how she died, a prestigious person could have been involved—one who did not wish to be found in the company of Cricket Coogler, and one who might be able to wield the power of his office to avoid detection.

Political observer Jack Flynn said he spoke to Governor John Sims, elected in 1955, about the case, and was told that when he (Sims) first entered the governor's office, the desk had been completely cleaned out. Not even a paper clip was left. But on the desktop lay one file, labeled "Cricket Coogler." Sims told Flynn he looked in it and then put it away, because his first thought was "My Lord, can you imagine the embarrassment to certain individuals if this file were ever made public?" Flynn said he tried for years to locate the Sims file, but it was not to be found (VI).

Every person named in this book, and hundreds unnamed, were affected by Cricket Coogler's death. The two grand juries convened because of her death became conduits of action in the form of indictments against several men—many with status and prestige in New Mexico. Efforts to coerce a confession to her murder had long-reaching effects, including lost jobs and damaged reputations. Powerful underworld figures chose to leave New Mexico and opted for Nevada. An out-of-power political party suddenly catapulted its candidate into the governor's chair. The turnover of dozens of political appointments began.

As time goes by, it becomes less and less likely that there are persons still living who know what really happened to Cricket Coogler. But it also remains likely that one or more told someone what they knew. Many people wish that the story would go away, that the families could be left alone—an understandable and humane impulse continuously expressed since 1949. Las Cruces Mayor Sam Klein said in a November 5, 1950, radio speech in Albuquerque that he and his town would like to forget about the Cricket Coogler murder case, and that Ed Mechem should never have brought the case into the campaign with a promise to solve it. Mayor Klein also mentioned that Happy Apodaca, Hubert Beasley, and Roy Sandman had been convicted for overzealousness (*SFNM* and *LCSN*, November 5, 1950). Victim Wesley Byrd and a federal jury held a different view of that "overzealousness."

Byron Darden answered Mayor Klein this way: "It would be a gross miscarriage of justice to muzzle the public demand for a solution to this murder. . . . Publicity on the Coogler case is not going to die and should not die until it is solved" (*LCSN*, November 5, 1950).

To forget Cricket Coogler, to bury what little is known and even guessed by those close enough to the circumstances to make educated guesses, seems too similar to the rationalization of those who hid the facts in 1949. There is a saying that justice favors the unforgotten.

It is not difficult to imagine Cricket Coogler, if she had survived, as a woman in her seventies who might say very little about what happened to her when she was young. At the end of her life, perhaps she would be remembered only by her family and friends. But her life was destined to end early, violently, unjustly, and publicly. Her presence remains vivid for all who study this case, both as a fascinating crime mystery and a useful political study. At a press conference in 2000, Walt Finley described the case by saying, "It's a part of our national history, including as it does the first civil rights case against law enforcement officers, and certainly a vital part of state history" (VI).

The case of Cricket Coogler remains the most prominent, the most damning, the most complicated, and the most interesting unsolved mystery in twentieth-century New Mexico. If it can be continually warmed by books and films and articles and essays, one day its solution may be "rendered," that is, purified by the process of melting, then heating slowly until as much certainty as possible has been extracted.

Acknowledgments

Although a complete list of source material follows, this book is based extensively on a few primary sources that deserve special recognition:

Reporter Walt Finley's coverage of the case in the *El Paso Herald-Post*, as well as coverage in the *Las Cruces Sun-News*, *Las Cruces Citizen*, and other newspapers, provided the foundation of the story and hundreds of essential details.

A Federal Bureau of Investigation file in the U.S. National Archives and Records Administration, Department of Justice, College Park, Maryland, provided extensive declassified documents. The focus of the file was the federal case concerning the torture of suspect Wesley Byrd, but many peripheral and vital reports having to do with the Coogler case in general were contained there.

The full-length video *The Silence of Cricket Coogler* (Trespartes Films, 2000), made by director Charlie Cullin, former New Mexico Film Commission head; editor Richard Startzman, award-winning cinematographer; narrator John Ehrlichman; commentators Jack Flynn and Tony Hillerman, and others, provided both a story guideline and fascinating on-camera interviews with individuals about the case. This documentary won the 2000 Axiem Award for Best Documentary in electronic form. Charlie Cullin also generously loaned his collection of uncut original videos from which *The Silence of Cricket Coogler* was compiled, and any reference to a videotaped interview means the source was that video and/or one of its outtakes. Digital Solutions of Las Cruces produced still photos from the video.

The papers of William Byron Darden at the Darden Law Firm, P.A., in Las Cruces, New Mexico, provided correspondence, handwritten notes, and other critical information.

Privileged interviews with generous people in Las Cruces and Doña

Ana County were invaluable. Even though some conversations began with "I don't think I can help you very much," so often they not only helped a great deal themselves but also recommended and introduced me to other knowledgeable sources.

Forensic anthropologist Dave Weaver provided extraordinary insights from his expert view in e-mail correspondence and an in-person interview (April 29, 2004) in Las Cruces. His suggested plausible explanations regarding the condition of Cricket Coogler's body were especially appreciated.

For valuable editing, support, and encouragement, I want to thank Leon Moore, Scott Moore, John Moore, Ann Rohovec, Kevin McIlvoy, Bill Conroy, Ray Sadler, Leora Zeitlin, Debbi LaPorte, and Beth O'Leary.

—Paula Moore

APPENDIX I
Cricket's Last Evening—Possible Timeline

DATE	TIME		SOURCE
March 30, 1949	3:00 p.m.	Cricket Coogler finishes shift at DeLuxe Café.	Bob Ash, *EPHP* 5/11/51
	4:00–6:00 p.m.	Cricket stays downtown, seen alone at the Del Rio Bar. Former boyfriend Lauren Welch spots her about 6:00 p.m. still downtown in her waitress uniform.	Finley, *EPHP* 5/23/49; Welch, NARA1
	6:15–7:00 p.m.	Cricket walks home, changes clothes, tells her mother she has a date but will not say with whom. She leaves home about 7:00 p.m.	Ollie Coogler, *EPHP* 5/23/49 and 6/27/51
	Hour unknown	An unidentified waitress says she served Dan Sedillo dinner in Las Cruces. Chope Benavides says Dan Sedillo was "around" that night.	Finley, *EPHP* 7/23/49; Benavides VI
	8:00 p.m.	Cricket is seen walking unsteadily on street in front of the DeLuxe Café.	Finley, *EPHP* 5/23/49
	9:00 p.m.	Luther "Mr. Green Eyes" Mosley encounters Cricket in the DeLuxe.	Mosley, *EPHP* 5/12/49
	9:00–9:30 p.m.	They return to the Tortugas Café, where Cricket is now served coffee and toast and promises to go home after she eats. A cop with slight build, possibly Lucero or Flores, talks to Cricket as Mosley pays bill.	Mosley, *EPHP* 5/12/49; Flores, *EPHP* 6/26/51

DATE	TIME		SOURCE
	9:30 p.m.	Cricket talks to DeLuxe manager Bob Ash, walks over to Del Rio Bar, talks with bartender there.	Finley, *EPHP* 5/23/49
	Between 10:00–11:00 p.m.	Cricket knocks over her drink in Del Rio Bar, just as Mosley rejoins her. She is not concerned about the spill damaging her suit, saying she will never live to wear it again anyway.	Fischer, *EPHP* 5/10/49
	10:30 p.m.	Mosley tries to buy Cricket coffee at Tortugas Café. Service to her is refused because she is drunk.	Mosley, *EPHP* 5/11/51
	10:45 p.m.	Mosley and Cricket order coffee and doughnuts at the Union Bus Depot, then return one block north to the Tortugas Café/bus station.	Finley, *EPHP* 5/23/49; Mosley, 6/26/51
	11:30 p.m.	Mosley and Cricket are back in the Del Rio Bar, where Mosley pays for more drinks.	Finley, *EPHP* 5/23/49
	Around midnight?	Mosley sees Jerry Nuzum and Cricket leave the Del Rio and go to Jerry's car. Mosley goes outside as Cricket jumps out of Nuzum's car, and Nuzum grabs her as if to put her back into the car. Mosley intervenes and the two men exchange testy words.	Mosley, *EPHP* 5/12/49 and 6/26/51
March 31, 1949	12:00–12:30 a.m.	After asking Shorty Fischer to make a call for her, Cricket makes a phone call herself to Joel Coffey and invites him to join her at the DeLuxe Café. He declines. She returns to the bar and cries.	Fischer, *EPHP* 5/10/49; J. Coffey, *EPHP* 7/21/49; Mosley *EPHP* 5/12/49

DATE	TIME		SOURCE
	1:00 a.m.	Cricket and Mr. Green Eyes leave the Del Rio and return to the DeLuxe.	Fischer, *EPHP* 5/11/49
	1:30 a.m.	Cricket and Mr. Green Eyes are back in the Del Rio Bar. Nuzum invites Cricket to play shuffleboard and they play until the bar closes.	Mosley, *EPHP* 5/11/49; Nuzum, *EPHP* 5/7/49
	2:00 a.m.	As the Del Rio closes, Shorty Fischer sees Cricket in the DeLuxe Café. Mosley joins her there. Cricket moves to a booth; Nuzum comes in and joins her there.	Fischer, *EPHP* 5/10/49
	2:15 a.m.	Nuzum pretends to make a call asking for authority to arrest a "woman who's been making trouble."	Mosley and Nuzum, *EPHP* 5/11/51
	2:30 a.m.	Nuzum makes a second attempt to put Cricket in his car. Mrs. Bob Ash arrives by bus at 2:20, walks about a block north, sees Cricket struggling with a man, sees her husband go out to them.	Mrs. Ash, *EPHP* 5/6/49
	2:30 a.m.	Bob Ash goes out to Nuzum's car to intervene. Cricket again heads back into the DeLuxe, and the two men go inside the café as well.	Bob Ash, *EPHP* 5/6/49
	About 3:00 a.m.	Nuzum leaves the DeLuxe alone, then Cricket leaves alone, then Mosley leaves to follow Cricket.	B. Ash and Mosley, *EPHP* 5/11/51
	2:55 a.m.	Landlady observes Nuzum's arrival at home, honking his horn under her window. He is assisted inside by his wife Mary, who confirms Nuzum is drunk.	Eloise Ellis, *EPHP* 4/6/51; Mary Nuzum, *EPHP* 6/29/51

DATE	TIME		SOURCE
	About 3:00 a.m.	Mary Foy says she sees two officers struggling with Cricket in a bus parking lot, where they hit her three times and dump her in a black state police car.	Foy, *EPHP* 6/29/51
	About 3:00 a.m.	W. C. McBride gets out of a taxi on corner of May and Church, sees Cricket on May, then on Church, sees official plates on a light gray or yellow car parked on the south side of May Street near Church.	McBride, *EPHP* 6/28/51
	3:05 a.m.	Officers Flores and Lucero see Cricket at corner of Main and Griggs, near vicinity of the post office and the Western Union office.	Vicente Lucero, *LCSN* 5/13/49
	After 3:00 a.m.	Mr. Green Eyes Mosley sees a car, dark gray or dark brown, driven by a man wearing a hat. He says the car almost hits Cricket on Main Street as she crosses it heading north toward Griggs.	Mosley, *EPHP* 5/12/49
	3:10–3:25 a.m.	Cricket appears to wait on corner of May and Church, then starts walking south on Church. She falls and quickly gets to her feet. A car passes her, turns in front of her, and she gets in. Luther Mosley says it might be the same car that almost hit Cricket a few minutes earlier.	Vicente Lucero, *LCSN* 5/13/49; Mosley, *EPHP* 5/12/49
	3:30 a.m.	McBride enters Gateway Gardens for a few minutes. When he comes out, Cricket is gone.	McBride, *EPHP* 6/28/51

DATE	TIME		SOURCE
March 31, 1949	No time given	Las Cruces waitress Katie Etherton may have served Sedillo breakfast the morning of March 31, but she appears confused as to the date, citing a Sunday morning instead of a Thursday.	Katie Etherton videotaped interview
March 31, 1949	No time given	A Las Cruces service station attendant says he serviced a state official's car on March 31, 1949, and presents a state charge slip for the man's signature. He says the state official had been drinking.	Finley, *EPHP* 6/20/49 and 7/23/49
March 31, 1949	Early afternoon	Happy Apodaca arrives in Albuquerque with companion Aurelia McFarland and two girls he is delivering to the Welfare Home.	B. Perkins, *EPHP* 5/28/49
March 31, 1949	Early afternoon	Jerry Nuzum arrives in Albuquerque with his wife, having withdrawn from NMA&M College and packed all household goods.	Bill Nuzum, *EPHP* 4/7/51
April 1, 1949	1:30 a.m.	Lauren Welch boards a bus for Kansas and is separated from his wife.	NARA1
ADDITIONAL DATES RELEVANT TO THE CASE			
April 6, 1949		Apodaca announces publicly the disappearance of Cricket Coogler.	*LCSN* 4/6/49
April 15, 1949		Sid Howard finds first shoe on west side of Highway 80/85.	*LCSN* 5/17/49
April 16, 1949		Four young rabbit hunters find the body of Cricket Coogler in the desert near Mesquite Cemetery.	*LCSN* 4/18/49

DATE	TIME		SOURCE
April 17, 1949		M. O. Johnson turns in second shoe he had been holding since he found it on April 4, 1949.	*LCSN* 4/18/49; *EPHP* 5/11/49
April 19, 1949		Wesley Byrd is arrested and, after some time, charged with selling a car (reportedly his own) without a dealer's license.	*LCSN* 4/20/49; *EPHP* 5/10/49
April 28, 1949		Wesley Byrd is taken to the site where Cricket Coogler's body was found and tortured in order to coerce his confession to her murder.	NARA transcript of Byrd's statement, *et al.*
About May 5, 1949		Jerry Nuzum is jailed at the Doña Ana County Courthouse without charge.	*LCSN* 5/5/49; *EPHP* 5/9/49
May 7, 1949		The body of Cricket Coogler is exhumed and examined.	*LCSN* 5/8/49
May 10, 1949		District attorney T. K. Campbell announces the release and exoneration of Jerry Nuzum. Walt Finley breaks the story about the torture of Wesley Byrd.	*EPHP* 5/10/49
May 18, 1949		Doña Ana County Grand Jury convenes, and after about three weeks bars Judge Scoggin and District attorney T. K. Campbell from its proceedings. Then it immediately begins to issue indictments.	*LCSN* 5/18/49; R. A. Durio videotaped interview
June 8, June 17, and June 24, 1949		Happy Apodaca is accused of rape by a Canadian woman visiting Las Cruces, and two young girls, both employed at the home of Joe De Turo at separate times, accuse Apodaca as well—one with a rape charge, the other with a seduction charge.	*EPHP* 6/8/49; Darden Papers

DATE	TIME		SOURCE
June 23, 1949		Doña Ana County Grand Jury and deputy sheriffs raid gambling houses simultaneously.	*EPHP* 6/24/49
July 1, 1949		Apodaca is ousted as sheriff pending removal trial.	*LCSN* 7/1/49
July 21, 1949		It is recognized in the press that Wesley Byrd has left Las Cruces, his whereabouts unknown.	*EPHP* 7/21/49
Aug. 6, 1949		Dan Sedillo denies morals charges in his indictment. Cricket Coogler is named as the female minor involved.	*LCSN* 8/5/49
Sept. 12–17, 1949		Apodaca's removal trial in Silver City, NM. Most of the charges are dismissed, then the judge declares a mistrial because of a deadlocked jury.	*LCSN* 9/15/49; *EPHP* 9/17/49
Oct. 11, 1949		Apodaca resigns and all charges against him, criminal and civil, are dropped.	*EPHP* 10/12/49; *LCC* 10/13/49
Nov. 7, 1950		Republican candidate Edwin L. Mechem is elected governor.	*LCSN* 11/8/50
Nov. 9, 1949– Jan. 5, 1950		Sedillo trial on morals charges begins in Las Cruces. Christmas holidays and lengthy interruption due to contempt charges intervene. Verdict: not guilty.	*EPHP* 11/10/49; *LCC* 1/5/50
Nov. 19, 1949		The Doña Ana County Grand Jury adjourns, having issued twenty-eight indictments throughout its May–November meeting. In its final report, the grand jury criticizes eight other public officials.	*EPHP* 11/19/49
June 7, 1950		Viramontes defeats Apodaca for sheriff in election.	*LCC* 6/7/50

DATE	TIME		SOURCE
July 13, 1950		Torture of Wesley Byrd reported in newspapers. Warrents are issued for Apodaca, Beasley, Sandman, and Sandoval.	*EPHP* 7/13/50
Sept. 18–22, 1950		"Torture Trial" of defendants Apodaca, Beasley, and Sandman in Santa Fe. Apodaca and Beasley are found guilty of violation of civil rights of another; Sandman guilty of conspiracy to violate same civil rights.	*AJ* 9/22/50
April 5, 1951		Nuzum is arrested in Pennsylvania.	*LCSN* 4/8/51
May 11, 1951		Nuzum hearing gets under way. Ollie Coogler attends. Happy Apodaca also attends.	*LCSN* 5/11/51
June 14, 1951		Apodaca and Sandman enter prison to begin one-year sentences at La Tuna Federal Correctional Farm near El Paso, TX (Beasley entered La Tuna the previous week).	*EPHP* 6/14/51
June 26–30, 1951		Nuzum trial in Las Cruces. A directed verdict of acquittal.	*AJ* 6/30/51

AJ = Albuquerque Journal
EPHP = El Paso Herald-Post
LCC = Las Cruces Citizen
LCSN = Las Cruces Sun-News

APPENDIX II
The Many Colored Cars

The Coogler case was all about cars: some Cricket jumped from, some politicians were driving, one that policemen could not start, a flashy new maroon sedan, taxis, coupes, and pickup trucks. The colors of the cars described were cream, yellow, almost black, black with a gold police insignia, dark gray, light gray, light blue, blue-green, dark blue, maroon, and brown, as well as a green pickup. Here is a recap of some cars, with their owners or their observers, taken from information in the Darden Papers, the *Las Cruces Sun-News*, the *Las Cruces Citizen*, the *El Paso Herald-Post*, as well as in Department of Justice files in the National Archives and Records, College Park, Maryland, and in *The Silence of Cricket Coogler*, Trespartes Films, 2000.

Jerry Nuzum's 1949 maroon Mercury, plate number 5–3030.

Wesley Byrd's 1937 Plymouth or Mercury, four-door, license plate 7–526. The dashboard was blue, so the car likely was as well. On May 7, 1949, a deputy, perhaps speaking of Byrd's car to a *Sun-News* reporter, said, "We have a car that is believed to be connected with the case." He was asked, "Do you have the owner of the car in custody?" He replied, "Not the owner." Since Byrd sold his car several days following Cricket's disappearance and was charged with selling a car without a dealer's license, the deputy could duck the question since Byrd no longer owned the car.

The following news-story reference also might have referred to Byrd's car: "A car brought in early last week is now believed to have a definite connection with the pretty young waitress' desert slaying. The vehicle is in a Las Cruces garage" (*LCSN*, May 7, 1949). On May 8, a *Las Cruces Sun-News* reporter asked T. K. Campbell whether any car besides Nuzum's had been impounded, and Campbell responded, "No comment."

Lauren Welch's 1939 four-door Oldsmobile, cream color, which he said was repossessed two weeks prior to March 31, 1949.

Jack ——'s: Lauren Welch said that a "grey-headed guy called Jack," who once allegedly wanted to marry Cricket, drove a 1937 gunmetal gray Lincoln Zephyr coupe.

Freddy Barncastle's 1941 or 1942 gray Chevy with a blue top. Former border patrol officer Sylba Bryant said policemen told him they had established the car Cricket got into—a 1941 gray two-tone Chevy—but could not put a driver in it.

Happy Apodaca's 1949 Packard, license 7–2507, possibly the same car in July 1950 from which Apodaca was asked to remove a red light, since he was no longer sheriff. The color is unknown.

William Love's (the man first suspected of the A&M Business Office robbery) 1947 Oldsmobile convertible, color unknown, which he said his sister gave him.

Police vehicles: Even the local police seemed to be switching cars. Captain John Moore of the Las Cruces Police Department said that when policemen Vincent Lucero and Ruben Flores picked him up on the morning of March 31, as their shift ended, they were driving a black Chevrolet owned by the police department. However, Captain Moore said a patrolman named Dallas Jackson had been assigned to that patrol wagon that night. If Cricket Coogler was put into the back seat of a police car, state or city, unconscious or dead, apparently no evidence was sought or found.

Car observed by Mary Foy: Foy described a black police car with gold insignia and lights on the top, from which she said two policemen emerged and beat Cricket Coogler, then loaded her into the back seat and drove away.

Car observed by Mr. Green Eyes Mosley: Mosley said Cricket spoke to two men in a dark gray or dark brown car as it almost struck her on Main Street, then saw the same car turn off Main onto Church Street. Two years later he said he thought the car was black.

Car observed by two city policemen, Vicente Lucero and Reuben Flores. They initially were quoted in newspapers as saying they saw Cricket enter a light gray or blue car, or, in another story, a blue-green car. But in a written statement published later, Lucero said the car was cream-colored.

Car observed by Katie Etherton: Waitress Etherton, who once worked with Cricket, said the night Cricket disappeared, she (Etherton) got off work at 2:00 a.m., and a customer and his girlfriend gave her a ride home. They observed a car being towed out of a garage not far from Katie's house. Katie said a politician owned that garage and she thought it odd that a car would be towed at that hour. She said she heard the car was from Hatch and the garage owner had been "storing it." The license number linked to that car was 7–3212. She did not say the color of the car. Etherton said she told Byron Darden about that car, but as far as she knew, no investigation followed.

The type of garage mentioned by Katie Etherton as belonging to a politician is uncertain. Perhaps Katie used the term "garage" to mean an auto-repair place. A few such "garages" along likely routes to her home were listed in the 1948 directory: the Cactus Motor Company at 228 S. Main; Cruces Motor Parts Company at 115 W. Bowman (quite near the Tortugas Café); Roark Garage at 320 S. Main; and Aztec Garage at 302 S. Main (the address in the 1948 Las Cruces directory is 236 North San Pedro). Perhaps Katie referred to a garage privately owned by a politician. Alberto Gutierrez, a Democratic Party leader and proprietor of the Palms Liquor Store on Main Street, lived in the same block as Katie Etherton. (Gutierrez was indicted by the Doña Ana County Grand Jury on a charge of operating gambling equipment. He pleaded guilty and was given a suspended sentence.)

Pickup: A green Chevrolet or International pickup observed by Robert Estrada on the evening of April 1, 1949, as a woman in a gray suit was hit by two men and dumped into the back. His report drew no response from law enforcement.

Car described as state vehicle: Tony Hillerman says in the video that he was told about a state car checked out to Lt. Governor Montoya or member(s) of his staff. No description of the car was published, but Hillerman says a car matching a description of the state car mysteriously burned in Roswell, New Mexico.

Car burned at "A" Mountain: About five days after Cricket Coogler disappeared, a burned car was also found near "A" Mountain (a Las Cruces landmark), but the local news reported neither the specific date the car was found, the make, model, or year. This brief statement may have reflected all the reporter could glean about this burned car: "Any connection between the [Coogler] murder and the finding of a burning car near 'A' Mountain was discounted after a complete investigation" (*LCSN*, May 5, 1949).

Robert Templeton's 1941 cream-colored Chevrolet.

Other license plate numbers, with no links to makes or models, were noted in handwriting in the papers of attorney Byron Darden: 7–5198, 7–1354.

Bibliography

Archives and Manuscript/Photograph Collections

Archives of the Sixth Judicial District Court, Silver City, New Mexico. Case #12255 (*State of New Mexico v. A. L. Apodaca*)

Archives of the Third Judicial District Court, Las Cruces, New Mexico. Case #8482 and #8537 (*State of New Mexico v. Jerry Nuzum*); Case #8148 and #8149 (*State of New Mexico v. Dan Sedillo*); Case #08101 (*State of New Mexico v. Robert Templeton*), and 1951 microfilm divorce record Barncastle, Esther vs. Fred.

Dennis Chavez Papers, MSS 394 BC, box 394, Correspondence M, Center for Southwest Research, Zimmerman Library, University of New Mexico, Albuquerque, New Mexico.

Federal Bureau of Investigation, U.S. Department of Justice, National Archives at College Park, MD, record group 144–49–7 (declassified 9/24/04 Authority EO 10501 by JA). The file box contains miscellaneous papers and the following referenced FBI reports filed in 1949 and 1950:

- NARA1-Report AQ [Albuquerque, NM] 44–2
- NARA2-Report CE [Charlotte, NC] 44–133
- NARA3-Report EP [El Paso, TX] 44–22
- NARA4-Report PG [Pittsburgh, PA] 44–55
- NARA5-Report 44–75 [No city designation]

Governor Thomas Mabry Papers, 1959–107, Carruthers State Records Center and Archives, Santa Fe, New Mexico.

New Mexico Department of Tourism Photo Collection, items 002562 and 002615, New Mexico State Records Center and Archives, Santa Fe, New Mexico.

Sheriff Jim Flanagan, Photograph Collection MS259, Rio Grande Historical Collection, Branson Library, New Mexico State University.

William B. Darden Papers, Darden Law Firm, P.A., Las Cruces, New Mexico.

Newspapers

Albuquerque Journal, Albuquerque, New Mexico.
El Paso Herald-Post, El Paso, Texas.
El Paso Times, El Paso, Texas.
Las Cruces Bulletin, Las Cruces, New Mexico.
Las Cruces Citizen, Las Cruces, New Mexico.

Las Cruces Sun-News, Las Cruces, New Mexico.
Las Cruces Sun-News: Celebrating 150 Years of Las Cruces History, special edition,
    October 9, 1999.
New York Times, New York, New York.
Santa Fe New Mexican, Santa Fe, New Mexico.

Government Documents

Apodaca v. US 188 F2d. 932 (1951), U.S. Code, Title 18, sections 371 and 3559, per legal
    researcher Joan Chavez, Albuquerque, NM.
New Mexico Secretary of State, New Mexico Blue Book, 1947–48. Date and place of
    publication not shown.
New Mexico Secretary of State, New Mexico Blue Book, 1949–50. Date and place of
    publication not shown.
U.S. Census Records (15th) 1930, Doña Ana County, New Mexico. Branigan Library,
    Las Cruces, NM.

Books

Beck, Warren A. A History of Four Centuries. Norman: University of Oklahoma Press,
    1962.
Caro, Robert A. Master of the Senate. New York: Alfred A. Knopf, 2002.
Espinosa, Gilberto, and Tibo, J. Chavez. El Rio Abajo. Ed. Carter Waid. Date and place
    of publication not shown.
Fincher, Ernest Barksdale. Spanish-Americans as a Political Factor in New Mexico,
    1912–1950. New York: Arno Press, 1974.
Historical Data Committee of the Centennial. History of Las Cruces and the Mesilla
    Valley. Las Cruces, NM, 1949.
Kirkpatrick, Mark, with Linda De La Torre and Deborah Gouldsmith. Las Cruces
    and Doña Ana County: A Pictorial History. Las Cruces, NM: Las Cruces Bulletin,
    Kilpatrick Newspapers, Inc., 1998.
Owen, Gordon. Las Cruces, New Mexico, 1849–1999: Multicultural Crossroads. Las
    Cruces, NM: Red Sky Publishing Co., 1999.
Vigil, Mario. Chicano Politics. Washington, DC: University Press of America, 1978.
Vigil, Mario. Political Leaders in New Mexico History. Washington, DC: University
    Press of America, 1980.
Welsh, Cynthia Secor. U.S. Army Corps of Engineers: Albuquerque District, 1935–1985.
    Albuquerque: University of New Mexico Press, 1987.

Articles

"Dead Men Tell Tales." Newsweek, May 11, 1953.
"National Affairs." Time, October 31, 1938.
"The Winner of No Election." Time, March 22, 1954.

Film

Cullin, Charlie, director. The Silence of Cricket Coogler, Trespartes Films, 2000.
    Narrated by John Ehrlichman. On-camera interviews with:

- Chope Benavides, restaurant and bar owner, friend of Happy Apodaca
- Sylba Bryant, former border patrol officer
- R. A. Durio, member of Doña Ana County Grand Jury
- Mary Durio, wife of R. A. Durio
- Walt Finley, newspaper reporter for *El Paso Herald-Post*, nominated for the Pulitzer Prize for his coverage of the case
- Jack Flynn, political columnist
- Alice Gruver, newspaper reporter for *El Paso Herald-Post* and UPI, wife of *Las Cruces Citizen* editor Homer Gruver
- Tony Hillerman, author with special interest in the case
- Dan Maddox, physician who first examined Cricket Coogler's body
- Jerry Nuzum, Pittsburgh Steeler, tried for the murder of Cricket Coogler
- Joe Pino, port of entry officer
- Sharon Thurber Johnson, stepdaughter of Roy Sandman
- Allen Russell Soper, member of Doña Ana County Grand Jury

Cullin, Charlie, director. Outtakes from *The Silence of Cricket Coogler*. Trespartes Films, 2000. Includes unused portions of on-camera interviews listed above, as well as an interview with Katie Etherton, a waitress and friend of Cricket Coogler, no portion of which was used in the final film.
"New Detectives: Case Studies in Forensic Science." Discovery Channel, June 19, 2004.

Reference Works

New Mexico Con Survey Directory, 1948. Columbus, OH: Mullin-Kille Company.
New Mexico Con Survey Directory, 1951. Columbus, OH: Mullin-Kille Company.
Telephone Directory, March 1946, for Las Cruces and Hatch. El Paso, TX: Mountain States Telephone and Telegraph Company.

Correspondence

Adams, Roger C., U.S. Pardon Attorney, U.S. Department of Justice, Washington, DC. July 28, 2004 (to author).
Hardy, David M., Records Management Division, U.S. Department of Justice, Federal Bureau of Investigation. May 27, 2005 (to author).
Hunt, Wanda M, Chief, Freedom of Information/Privacy Office, U.S. Department of Justice, Federal Bureau of Prisons. September 30, 2004 (to author).
O'Rourke, Marie A., Assistant Director, U.S. Department of Justice, Executive Office for United States Attorneys. August 6, 2004, August 31, 2004, and February 25, 2005 (to author).
Weaver, Dave, Forensic Anthropologist and Professor Emeritus, Wake Forest University (to author).
Wiggins, Janice, U.S. National Archives and Records Administration, Washington, DC. February 2004 (phone call to author).

Web Sites

"Alcohol Poisoning," Wikipedia. http://en.wikipedia.org. February 25, 2006.

Calloway, Larry. "Cultures Color New Mexico Politics." *Albuquerque Journal* online, September 19, 1999. www.abqjournal.com.

Matray, James I. "Joseph Manuel Montoya." American National Biography Online. www.anb.org/articles. January 17, 2004.

National Governors Association. www.nga.org. Biographical information re Governors Mabry and Mechem. July 7, 2007.

State v. Bailey, 62 N.M. 111, 305 P.2d 725. www.fastcase.com.

U.S. Social Security Death Index. www.social_security_death_index_search.com. Last accessed July 6, 2007.

Author Interviews (except for those persons who requested anonymity)

Berg, Jeff, host of a 2004 showing of *The Silence of Cricket Coogler*. June 3, 2004, Las Cruces, New Mexico.

Bradford, Cedric, friend of Wesley Byrd in 1949 (later the first black foreman of a federal grand jury). April 30, 2004, Las Cruces, New Mexico.

Caldwell, Meredith Malone, Las Cruces resident in 1949. April 19, 2004, Las Cruces, New Mexico.

Darden, John, son of attorney Wm. B. Darden (hired by the Doña Ana County Grand Jury). July 1, 2004, Las Cruces, New Mexico.

Durio, R. A., member of Doña Ana County Grand Jury, and his wife Mary and son Bobby. April 16, 2004, Las Cruces, New Mexico.

Fielder, Clarence, Las Cruces resident in 1949. January 5, 2005, Las Cruces, New Mexico.

Ford, Quentin, New Mexico A&M student in 1949. April 12, 2004, Las Cruces, New Mexico.

Foreman, Jeanneice, Doña Ana County resident in 1949. August 27, 2003, La Mesa, New Mexico.

Garcia, Willie, retired New Mexico state policeman. August 3, 2004, Las Cruces, New Mexico.

Griffith, Ollie, Doña Ana County resident in 1949. August 27, 2003, La Mesa, New Mexico.

Holguin, Mel, Las Cruces city policeman in 1949. April 13, 2004, Las Cruces, New Mexico.

Johnston, Edna, Doña Ana County resident in 1949. October 24, 2004, and November 10, 2004, Mesilla, New Mexico.

Marquez, Art, Las Cruces resident in 1949. June 24, 2004, and July 20, 2004, Las Cruces, New Mexico.

Maveety, Bob, Las Cruces resident in 1949. Fall 2003, Las Cruces, New Mexico.

Noble, Robert, Las Cruces paperboy in 1949. March 24, 2004, Las Cruces, New Mexico.

Pearson, Cissy Lara (via Betty Muncrief), resident of Mesquite in 1949. August 27, 2003, Las Cruces, New Mexico.

Peña, Josie, Las Cruces resident in 1949. April 13, 2004, Las Cruces, New Mexico.

Peters, Bill, retired FBI agent. July 5, 2007, Albuquerque, New Mexico.

Porter, Bob, New Mexico A&M student in 1949. May 4, 2004.

Sharpe, Connie, secretary to district attorney T. K. Campbell in 1949. November 19, 2004, Las Cruces, New Mexico.

Smith, Jerry, the first of the teenage rabbit hunters in 1949 to find Cricket Coogler's body. May 13, 2004, Anthony, New Mexico.

Uttley, Molly W., Las Cruces resident in 1949. June 22, 2004, Las Cruces, New Mexico.

Weaver, Dave, forensic anthropologist. April 29, 2004, Las Cruces, New Mexico.

Index

at Apodaca's removal trial, 93; request of second test of blood/skin by, 111–12

Milkman, Robert, 54–55, 84, 159; payoff allegations against, 85–86

Montoya, Joseph, 75; as lieutenant governor, 16, 57, 80–83, 122–23, 156–57; payoff allegations against, 85; state car of, 195; as U.S. Representative/Senator, 171–74

Mosley, Luther "Mr. Green Eyes," 20, 22–28, 51, 109, 114–15, 157–58; car observed by, 194

New Mexico, 65

New Mexico A&M College, 2–3; burglary at, 58–59, 98, 116, 155–56, 159

Nuzum, Jerry, 20–29, 34, 100–118, 157–59, 161–62, 174; 1949 arrest of, 102–7; 1951 trial of, 108–18; car of, 102–6, 193

Nuzum, Mary, 28, 58, 101, 103–5, 108, 110–11

Oman, LaFel, 30, 56, 83, 93, 134, 161

Ramirez, Sheriff Santos, 15, 55; Doña Ana County Grand Jury criticizes, 60; payoff allegations against, 85

Rife, Dr. Dwight, 111–12, 158

Salas, Carlos, 114–15, 130, 132–33, 147, 159, 175; Doña Ana County Grand Jury criticizes, 60; payoff allegations against, 84–85; and "Torture Trial," 135, 142–45

Salazar, I. E. "Sally," 114–15, 124–25, 130, 147, 152, 160; Doña Ana County Grand Jury criticizes, 60; indictment of, 133; payoff allegations against, 56; and "Torture Trial," 134, 138–39, 143–44

Salazar, Victor, 76, 85–86, 119, 160–61, 171, 175; and Bureau of Revenue, 81–83

Sandman, Roy, 17–18, 78, 94, 98, 118, 131, 175–76; at Apodaca's trial, 84; and

Connie Sharpe, 154; indictment of, 133; resignation of as deputy, 89; and "Torture Trial," 134–48, 166

Scoggin, Judge W. T. Jr., 18, 51, 54–57, 71, 109, 170, 176; barred from Doña Ana Grand Jury proceedings, 56; convenes grand jury, 52; Doña Ana Grand Jury criticizes, 60; payoff allegations against, 85–86

Sedillo, Dan, 34, 92, 119–27, 156, 161, 176–77; as corporation commissioner, 16, 81, 171–72; and Cricket Coogler, 83, 94, 152; Doña Ana County Grand Jury appearance of, 57, 120; indictment of, 59, 62, 120–21; trial of, 121–27

Sedillo, Rufus, 94, 122, 124–26, 172, 177

Smith, Glenn, 36–37

Smith, Jerry, 36–38, 72

Soper, Allen, 14, 17, 53–54, 57, 120, 156

Sunland Club, 54–56, 84. See also Marcus, Barney

Sunland Park. See Anapra

T-1, T-2, T-3: as confidential FBI informants, 55, 84–86, 143

Tafoya, Ernest "Tuffy," 55, 80, 108, 110–11

Talamantes, Josie, 9–10, 106

Templeton, Robert, 49, 161–62; car of, 195

Tropics. See Marcus, Barney; Sunland Club

Utz, Nolan, 41, 104, 113

Valley Country Club, 56–58, 84, 92–94, 159. See also Milkman, Robert

Viramontes, Joe Jr., 138

Viramontes, Sheriff Jose, 98–99, 147

Weaver, Dave, 44–47

Welch, Lauren, 8, 21, 32, 147, 163–64; car of, 193

White Sands Proving Grounds, vii, 3, 79, 82, 171